Halloween Crafts:
Eerily Elegant Decor

Kasey Rogers and Mark Wood

Published by
Krause Publications
300 E. State Street
Iola, Wisconsin 54990-0001
www.krause.com

Please call or write for our free catalog of publications. To place an order
or obtain a free catalog, call our toll-free number: 800-258-0929, or please
use our regular business telephone 715-445-2214.

Library of Congress Catalog Number 2001088592
ISBN 0-87349-291-9

Some products in this book are registered trademarks of their respective
companies:
FleckStone® by Plasti-Kote; DMC® Floss; Fimo®; Delta Renaissance Silver Foil Kit®; Instant Iron® and Instant Rust® by Modern Options; Dover
Art Clip Art®; X-Acto® Knives, WD-40®.

Photography:
Kasey Rogers
Mark Wood
Joseph Montegue

DEDICATION

To all the goblins, ghouls and ghosties that helped inspire our creepy little creations. And to all the witches, warlocks and other-worldlies who enriched our lives with magic (Samantha, Endora and Aunt Clara, our family physician, Dr. Bombay and our beloved babysitter, Esmerelda) we gratefully dead-icate this haunting little Hallowe'en book.

Oh—and to Mark's mom, Shirley, too.

CONTENTS

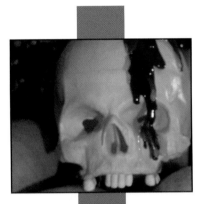

ACKNOWLEDGMENTS

Kasey and I would like to thank our many friends and the companies who helped make this book possible.

For providing us the with the most beautiful locations possible for photographing our crafts:

Sandra Hildebrandt, executive director of The Stagecoach Inn Museum; Glenda Reed, Shirley Wainess and Lacey Wainess of the White Meadows Art Gallery and the Francis Lederer Estate; Phyllis Power, museum director of The Motion Picture and Television Hospital; The Leonis Adobe & Plummer House.

And for supplying us with wonderful products:

Bruce Baum of Cesar, Inc.; GayLee Threadgill and Sue Barker of the Goelitz Candy Co.; Kinko's Copy Stores; Jeanne Stone of the OmniGlow Corp.; Michele Finnigan and Deb O'Shea of Plasti-Kote; Valspar Corp.

Special thanks to our friends at Hooper Camera, Calabasas, California.

And, some wonderful friends:

Julia del Judge, for the use of her truck in transporting tons of stuff; Doug Shephard for the use of his muscles in lifting lots of stuff. We would also like to thank our families, especially Shirley K. Wood for helping us to make all those danged Party Fans and Favors!

The Francis Lederer Estate

The picturesque Stagecoach Inn Museum is a Monterey-style building surrounded by four and one half acres of parks. First erected in 1876, it houses period rooms and special exhibits. The spacious grounds also feature a pioneer house, a rancho adobe, a fully-equipped carriage house and the 19th-century Timber School. The museum complex buildings are nestled around the slopes of a Conejo Valley creek and include gracious lawns studded with live oak trees, colorful seasonal flower gardens, wooded areas and a delightful arbored rose garden. The buildings and their displays tell the story of the early inhabitants of California and the Conejo Valley. The Museum is located just off the 101 freeway halfway between Los Angeles and Santa Barbara.

The Stagecoach Inn Museum

Pierre: Fact, Fiction or Fantasy?

The legend of Pierre the ghost has become a part of the lore at the Stagecoach Inn Museum. His "existence" was brought to light in the late 1960s when a psychic claimed she felt the presence of a ghost in the building. She said that in 1889 a thirty-five year old man had been shot while on the second floor of the Inn and that his name was Pierre Duvon or Duval. No other documentation confirms his life or death.

6

INTRODUCTION

It is the night of Hallowe'en
When all the witches may be seen
Some are fat
And some are lean
And some are as tall as a castor bean!

Remember that little song from childhood about Hallowe'en—a magical night when hobgoblins abounded, skeletons rattled, ghosts shrieked and witches swept cobwebs off the moon with their broomsticks? Hallowe'en was fun, then, and scary!

After years of working with the best of witches, I've learned that when decorating for Hallowe'en, things beautiful and elegant should be considered as well as what's fun and scary. Even though the traditional symbols of All Hallow's Eve are spooky, it can still be a surprisingly gorgeous holiday.

So, let's look at the bright side!

I'm thinking of that irresistible time of year when flame colored trees are everywhere afire, fields are plump with pumpkins, corn rustles in the shock and frosty evenings foretell the change of seasons. Now add the other sure signs of the season: dark and stormy nights, creaking tree limbs; mists in the dell, a graveyard full of wraiths and a distant howl shattering the all-too quiet night.

Now, that's Hallowe'en.

In the following pages, I and my friend and crafty conspirator, Mark, will combine the gracious and the ghoulish to help you turn your home into an inviting and enchantingly scary delight.

Imagine drippy, flickering electric candles to light your way through a haunted home, little red imps with green glowing eyes, banquets fit for the Goblin King and harvests of skulls. Plus, we've conjured up some tasty treats to serve your friends who are out and about on this "Beggar's Night!"

So get out those craft tools, tables and togs and let's settle in for some serious Hallowe'en "skull-duggery!" Who knows, some of these ghastly goodies may just turn out to be heirloom "kreep-sakes."

Best Witches,
Kasey Rogers
(Louise Tate of Bewitched)

... a few words from Mark:

Any great party rests on its guests, food and decoration ... the latter of which usually falls by the wayside. Well, you don't have to be a Martha Stewart and her "cast of thousands" to decorate your place with a frightening flare.

For instance, the table setting (or "BOO!-fey" as we like to call it) can be all-important since it is the main focus of a party. Not only should it hold the food and drink but also one's attention!

First, let's assemble a few basic tools to be used in crafting:

— Sewing machine
— Thread
— Hot glue gun
— Glue sticks
— Scissors
— Pinking shears
— Florist's wire
— Straight pins

Now, let's get ready for a little terror on the table top! Remember, read all instructions before beginning any craft project.

Mark

Hallowe'en Crafts: Eerily Elegant Decor

 chapter 1

HARVEST OF SKULLS

Full of the classic warm and vibrant autumn colors, the "Harvest of Skulls" is a wonderful and slightly macabre setting for any Hallowe'en Haunt.

Skull Orchard Statue

1 To make this bit of grave-yard art, first choose a stately plaster statue from an arts and crafts store, or nursery, for your centerpiece. We used a cherub, but a Greek goddess or gargoyle would be equally as effective. What ever it is, make sure it holds a bowl of some kind so you can build an arrangement in it later. Don't be afraid to let it tower above your dining room or coffee table. The taller it is, the more impressive, and leaves more table room for tricks or treats. (Ours stands a full 36" before the arrangement!)

2 Next, following package instructions, spray the statuary piece with the gray primer and let dry. Follow with the Manhattan Mist FleckStone. Again, let dry before giving a very light spritz of Gotham Gray. Let dry completely.

· 1 plaster statue with bowl

· FleckStone Spray kit, and other spray paints by Plasti-Kote:
   Gotham Gray
   Manhattan Mist
   Clear sealant
   Gray primer

· Moss green acrylic paint

· Black acrylic paint

· Spray bottle

· Sponge

11

3 Dilute the black paint with water and, using a spray bottle, lightly spray the statue, allowing the paint to run down in rivulets. Water down the moss green paint and lightly sponge into all of the statue's crevices. This will give it the look of having been moldering in a cemetery for ages.

4 When completely dry, spray with clear sealant.

Haunted Hint

This decoration may be used outside but should not be left outside. If it is, the FleckStone may fall off, the moss will disintegrate and the plaster statue could melt—then again, that might be perfect for Hallowe'en!

Creepy Drippy Candles

Skull Holder

Breathe new life into those old plastic electric Christmas candles sitting in your attic.

materials

- 1 single bulb, electric Christmas candle
- 1 flicker flame bulb
- Penny
- Glue gun
- Eleven 10" glue sticks (or more if desired; you can never have too much hot glue)
- Life-size plastic skull
- Aluminum foil
- Masking tape
- Black spray paint (or Hallowe'en color of choice)
- Small hand saw
- Drill with 1" bit

instructions

1 The glue gun needs to be really hot; you're going to be melting a lot of glue! Next, check all candles to make sure they work. Remove bulbs.

2 Break away the plastic base of the electric candle (unknotting the cord if necessary) and discard. Carefully saw the candle to desired length. *Be careful* not to cut through the cord.

3 Drill a 1" hole in the top of the skull and cover completely with aluminum foil. Closely conform the foil to skull. Thread the electric cord through the hole in the skull and stand the candle on top. Secure by dripping hot glue around the candle base.

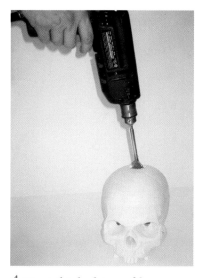

4 Start thick drips of hot glue near the base of the candle, allowing it to run down the hollows of the skull and

into its eyes and nose. It's okay to get glue on the cord.

5 Let this first layer dry before adding the next layer. Starting a little higher, drip more glue globs down the side of the candle. Continue in this manner until you've reached the top.

6 Allow the glue to run in natural rivulets down the side, just as wax on a real candle would.

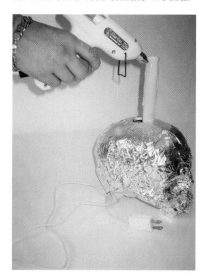

7 When glue is dry, take the candle and skull outside. Place a penny over the socket and spray with paint. Let dry.

8 When paint is completely dry, bring out the glue gun again. Drip some plain, uncolored glue from the top down. This will dry a little translucent making the melted "wax" appear to be fresh.

9 Remove the penny and peel away the foil. When done, replace the candle on top of the skull—the "wax" should conform to its features. You may wish to secure it with a little more hot glue.

10 Insert the flicker flame bulb and place the candle anywhere there's a plug and scream BOO!

13

Haunted Hints

Blowing on the hot glue as it drips will help control its path. Again, always let each layer dry before adding the next.

For the skull on the top of the statue, we used three electric candles cut to different heights and taped them together.

YET ANOTHER HAUNTED HINT: Be extra careful not to get any glue in a socket. If this does happen, go ahead and fill that one up. There's no going back. Then insert a small piece of toothpick into the still warm glue and color it black with a marker to resemble a wick. This will make it look like one of the candles blew out on a dark and stormy night!

Candle on Stack of Books

materials

· Several old books

· Hot glue

· Glue gun

· Aluminum foil

· Drill with 1" bit

· 1 single bulb, electric Christmas candle

instructions

1 Make a stack of several old books (we found ours on a used books store's dollar table) and hot glue together. Mark top book where the hole for the cord should be and drill through each book with 1" drill bit. Cover books with foil, thread candle cord through hole and let the gluing begin.

2 Break away the plastic base of the electric candle (unknotting the cord if necessary) and discard. For thin, dangling drips of "wax," glue a string onto the side so it hangs free. Drip hot glue down the string. This takes some practice but you really can't go wrong. The more glue, the creepier the candles!

Haunted Hint

YET ANOTHER HAUNTED HINT: Make a few puddles of painted hot glue to place on the floor under the dripping candles for an even more realistic look.

Candle Dripping Off Furniture

materials

- · Cardboard shoebox
- · Foil
- · Hot glue
- · Glue gun
- · I single bulb, electric Christmas candle
- · Paint (oranges are good)

instructions

1 Break away the plastic base of the electric candle (unknotting the cord if necessary) and discard. Cover a shoebox with foil. Set a candle or candles at its very edge. Put globs of hot glue directly onto the base of the candles, allowing them to drip down the front of the shoebox as far as desired.

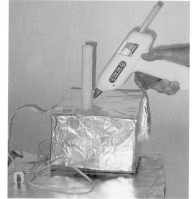

2 Once dry and painted, you can safely set the candles on the edge of any piece of furniture, making it look as though they have dripped all over it!

Harvest of Skulls

Candle in Holder

materials

- 1 short wooden candlestick from craft store
- Replacement electric plug from hardware store (the kind that easily clamps on)
- Drill with 1/2" bit
- Black paint
- 1 single bulb, electric Christmas candle

instructions

1 Drill a hole completely through a short, wooden candlestick top to bottom. Paint candlestick black.

2 Remove base from plastic candle (see instructions page 12) and cut short.

3 Clip plug from end of cord and feed through drilled hole in candlestick.

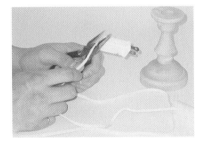

4 Follow package instructions and attach replacement plug. Hot glue (see instructions page 12). This candle will have to be painted by hand; otherwise the instructions are the same.

Harvest of Skulls Centerpiece

materials

- 5 life size plastic human skulls (2 with Creepy Drippy Candles)
- Two 6' red berry vines
- 5 orange Monster Glow Light-sticks by OmniGlow
- 1 small grapevine wreath (to fit bowl of Skull Orchard statue)
- Package of 6 florist's foam blocks
- Floral picks (or three-inch nails with heads)
- Fall foliage
- Artificial grapes in three or more colors, several bunches
- Spanish moss, 2 bags
- Silk red roses, 4 stems each with 1 rose and 1 rosebud
- Various gourds, apples, pomegranates and pumpkins
- Serrated knife

instructions

1 Fill the entire bowl of the statue with florist's foam, shaving it with a serrated knife to fit. Next, lightly drape the foam with enough Spanish moss to conceal the foam. Let some long tendrils hang down in front of the statue.

2 Place the grapevine wreath around the statue's bowl and then secure the skull with the candles to the foam with floral picks or nails. (Tape all electric cords discretely behind the statue.) If any florist's foam shows, add a bit more moss.

3 Starting at the top, secure and then twine the first berry vine loosely around the statue.

4 Clump the grapes in bunches of two and three and secure them to the foam with floral picks from underneath

so they hang down. (Don't cover the statue's face.)

5 Remove the jawbones from three other skulls (two regular and the third with a Creepy, Drippy Candle on its head). Stack them next to the statue's base. Wedge another block of florist's foam behind the top skull for added steadiness and cover with wisps of moss.

6 Pile pumpkins, gourds, pomegranates, grapes, and ap-ples around the skulls and statue and top with the other red berry vine.

7 Finally, tuck the fall foliage and roses around the entire arrangement, higher in the back and lower in the front. (Place a rose in the mouth of one of the skulls … it looks extra eerie!) It's best to use only one kind of autumn leaf; a little uniformity goes a long way to make a great arrange-ment.

8 When all of your arrange-ment building is done, snap and shake a Lightstick and slip it carefully inside each skull. They will glow eerily for hours.

9 Lastly, why not use another skull with a few gourds, ap-ples and leaves at the base of your sideboard or on an an-tique chair you don't want anyone sitting in (see photo on page 9)?

Haunted Hints

(see photo on page 9)

The berry vine comes rolled up but don't un-furl it too much. Allow it to coil and wind about.

Silk flowers and leaves almost always come on stems or bushes; don't use them like that. Pull them apart, using twigs and individual blossoms to fill in the arrange-ment.

YET ANOTHER HAUNTED HINT: For fun, insert several florist wires here and there in the arrangement, loaded with pieces of candy corn. They'll bob around and you and your guests can pick them out and eat them!

18

For a table centerpiece, find a tall, painted candlestick and build a skull arrangement on top. We first secured some florist's foam and another skull onto the top spike of the candlestick using floral pins. Next, wrap another berry vine up and around the skull. A few autumn leaves, grapes and left over pumpkins and there you have it: instant table centerpiece.

The worms crawl in,
the worms crawl out,
The worms crawl in
and out your snout!
They eat your eyes,
they eat your nose,
They eat the jelly
between your toes!

Harvest of Skulls

chapter 2

BANQUET OF THE GOBLIN KING

The Goblin King

materials

- 2 Hubbard squash (one larger than the other)
- 1/2 yard heavy white linen
- 4-1/2 yards of 2" wide sheer white lace
- 4 stone-colored felt squares
- 4 moss green felt squares
- 1 package iridescent sequins
- 6 faux pewter buttons
- 2 silver star buttons
- Hand saw
- Paring knife
- White thread
- Black thread
- Straight pins
- Pre-cut floral wire lengths, 1 package of 24
- Black poster board
- Delta Renaissance Silver Foil Kit
- Cotton string , 1 ball
- White glue
- Hot glue gun
- Polyester batting, 1 large bag
- Several 1" finishing nails
- Footed bowl large enough to hold biggest Hubbard squash

Let's take a detour from the usual orange and black regalia of a typical Hallowe'en and conjure up a "mid-evil" celebration in frosty greens and silver. Crowned this year's Lord of Misrule, the king of all the Goblins is ready to reign at your Hallowe'en party. Right: Mark finds the perfect Goblin King!

Banquet of the Goblin King

The Crown

instructions

1 First, make a pattern by measuring around the top of the smallest Hubbard squash where it begins to flare out, adding 1/2" to that measurement. Cut a strip of newspaper 5" wide by the measurement you took of the top of the squash. Divide the crown pattern top into six evenly-spaced points. (We used the bottom of a glass to get an even, curved line.) Cut out scallops and then trim 1/2" off points.

2 Next, cut the crown out of poster board, using the pattern you have just made. Dip three lengths of string into the white glue and, laying them side-by-side, outline the top and bot-

tom of the crown. Allow to dry. This will give the crown a look of stability.

3 Follow the instructions on the Delta Renaissance Silver Foil Kit to give the poster board crown a hammered-sil-

ver look. When dry, hot glue the crown into a circle and add a faux pewter button to the top of each point.

4 Dip the sequins in the white glue and "sprinkle" one at a time on the crown.

The Grande Ruff

instructions

1 Cut out two 5" x 45" strips from the white linen and stitch one end to the other, to make one, long strip. Open seam and press flat. Turn up a 1/4" seam twice along one side and press with a warm iron. Cut a 2-1/2 yard length of the white lace and sew to the pressed hem.

2 Use a running stitch to hand gather the ruff along the raw edge. Pull in to about 6". Stitch together into a circle and tie off. Run a length of

florist's wire through the small casing formed by the hem.

3 Shape with fingers as shown.

The Hands

instructions

1 Enlarge pattern provided (Pattern, page 111) to fill up an entire 8-1/2" x 11" sheet of paper. Cut two hand shapes from the stone felt and two from the moss green. Top stitch one of each color to the other, 1/4" from edge. Repeat for other hand. Note: these will not be turned right sides out.

2 Bend a length of florist's wire in half. Then bend each end down, forming a letter "M" shape. Insert the bent wire into the back two fingers. Repeat for next two fingers.

3 Stuff the fingers, thumbs and hands with batting (this is

also a great place to use up all those felt scraps instead of tossing them).

4 Cut the remaining lace in half (two 1 yard pieces) and

hand-gather the straight edge. Stitch to "wrist" part of glove.

5 Dip the sequins in the white glue and "sprinkle" one at a time on the hands.

The Boots

instructions

1 Enlarge boot pattern (Pattern, page 112) to fill an 8-1/2" x 11" sheet of paper and cut two of each color felt. Cut two boot bottoms from green felt. Top stitch boots according to pattern: point "A" to point "B" and point "C" to point "D." Next, top stitch boot bottoms into left over opening.

2 Stuff boots, add sequins and hand stitch a star button on each toe.

Assembling the Goblin King

instructions

1 Now, to assemble the big Goblin guy himself: Saw the top off the larger squash making it level. Discard top. Saw the top (be sure to keep this top) off the smaller squash, hollow out and carve a wickedly regal face.

2 Place larger squash in bowl (or saw its bottom off to level and set on a plate). Pin the ruff to body opening and then secure the head to the body by

inserting the rounded "chin" of head into hole in top of body. Push finishing nails through head and into body. The ruff should hide all raw edges. If it doesn't, add a few leaves and berries, as shown in the photo on page 21.

3 Pin the hands to the sides and the feet straight out from the bottom (so he looks as though he just plopped himself down in the middle of the festivities).

4 Put a candle in the Goblin King head and replace top of head, securing with finishing nails.

5 Set the crown at a jaunty angle on your Goblin King, or make a big "to do" out of the moment and hold his coronation that evening when your guests arrive. He'll really like that!

Haunted Hints

Dry ice placed in bowls of warm water and hidden behind your table arrangements will add just the right touch of the macabre.

Pull out all the good silver and use it! Polishing is unnecessary—the more tarnished, the better. After all, it's Hallowe'en.

Subjects of the Goblin King

What is a kingdom without a bunch of "merry men" to populate its court? Here, white pumpkins magically transform into an Elizabethan menagerie.

Banquet of the Goblin King

Bilious Candlesticks

materials

· Patina Green Antiquing Set by Modern Options (see Resources, page 125)

· Various candlesticks (metal, wood, ceramic, etc.)

instructions

1 This is a really simple project to do, but first you must spend some time collecting a menagerie of old, discarded candlesticks from thrift stores. You can also purchase inexpensive ones from craft supply and discount stores. Vary the heights to add more interest to your table. Make sure the candlesticks are clean and free of dirt and oils. Apply verdigris as directed on the Modern Options Kit.

Don't throw away those old silver-plated candlesticks that are loosing their luster. Help them to a new eerie formality by giving them an Old World verdigris finish.

Haunted Hint

We put the oxidizing fluid in a spray bottle and found this the easiest way to apply it. The more copper base you apply in the beginning, the better the candlestick will look.

The Tudor Ruff

materials

· 1/4 yard heavy white linen, 44" or 45" wide

· 1-1/4 yards white pearl on bias tape trim

· White thread

· Spray starch

· Iron

· Sewing machine with zipper foot

· Hand-sewing needle

instructions

1 Fold right sides of linen together lengthwise, sandwiching the white pearl trim between the linen, and machine-stitch using a zipper foot. Turn right sides out and carefully iron flat.

2 Heavily starch according to product instructions. Let dry.

3 With needle and thread, gather along the back and pull together. Stitch and tie off as before.

Goblin Masques
The Cocque Feather Masque

materials

- Various masks
- Delta Renaissance Silver Foil Kit*
- 3/4 yard silver cording
- 18 to 24 peacock feather eyes **
- 36 Cocque feathers dyed iridescent black**
- 2 Cocque feather tufts dyed iridescent black **
- 1 package green rocaille beads
- 1 package 1" long silver bugle beads
- 1 package black iridescent sequins
- Scrap of bias tape at least 7" long
- Black acrylic paint

* See Resources on page 125. One kit should complete two masks, as well as the crown of the Goblin King (shown on page 22.)

** (See Resources, page 125.)

instructions

1 Using hot glue, start at eye edges and cover mask with feathers, always over-lapping. Use longer ones on the center top. Outline eyes with silver sequins.

2 For the beadwork, double thread a needle and knot. Trim any loose ends from knot and slip on a green rocaille bead. Before it gets to the knot, slip needle between threads and pull. Bead is now secure.

3 Top rocaille bead with a long silver bugle bead, followed by 7 more rocaille beads. Repeat and top with bugle bead. Starting at one end of bias tape scrap, stitch and knot. There, one is done—only 59 to go! There are 60 strands hanging down from this mask.

4 When all are complete, hot glue bias tape to the inside, lower edge of mask (be sure to form into nose too) and trim any remaining threads.

Haunted Hint

If the beading for the Cocque Feather Masque is too much for you, or you simply don't have the time, use 6" of long black "flapper" fringe found in many fabric stores.

Silvered "Pinocchio" Masques

1 Follow the instructions on the Delta Renaissance Silver Foil Kit. When dry, paint a triangle of black acrylic paint underneath one eye (we used two of these masks and decorated opposite eyes for each).

2 Starting on one side, hot glue the silver cord around the edges. Cover the cord ends by hot gluing a Cocque feather tuft (pronounced "coke," a Cocque feather is just a fancy way of referring to a rooster tail feather) on the mask's side.

The Peacock Masque

instructions

1 Trim the fringed edges from 13 peacock feathers. Start at the corner of the eyes and hot glue the trimmed feathers around eye opening, overlapping slightly as you go. Glue one with fringe to center top of mask and two more with fringe on either side of it. Glue another one with fringe to hang down from tip of nose. Glue a trimmed feather onto either side of nose.

2 For the bridge of nose: tape the backside of a feather with masking tape and cut the bottom of the feather in a slightly upward curve. Form over bridge of nose and glue in place.

3 Use white glue and outline eyeholes with black iridescent sequins. One row on top, two on the bottom. Dot individual sequins around the feathers.

Putting Together the Loyal Subjects

instructions

1 Cut open the pumpkins *from the bottom* and scoop out the insides. (For the teardrop shaped hubbard, use the handsaw and cut off the bottom, leaving it level.)

2 Carve appropriate goblinesque faces in the pumpkins and squash. These need not be too elaborate as with all these ruffs and masks they will be quite "smashing" pumpkins on their own! A small hole cut in the back of each pumpkin with an apple corer will allow excess heat to escape and provide more oxygen for the candle flame.

3 Next, place the candle stubs into the candlesticks. Cut an "X" in the center of all the cake circles and cover them with foil. Push the candle up through the "X" in the circle and then press all down firmly onto the candlestick.

4 Place the ruff on next and set the pumpkin or squash on top of that.

5 Pin the masks in place. Further decorate with silver star-shaped sequin beauty marks pinned onto their faces.

6 Add a grand silver punch bowl with a bubbling brew so your merry men will feel more frolicsome.

materials

- Assortment of small, white "Luminaria" pumpkins and green Hubbard squash (one for every Bilious Candlestick and Tudor Ruff you made)
- Small hand saw
- Paring knife (smaller knives are sturdier than bigger ones for carving)
- Taper candle stubs (or taper candles cut about 3" to 4")
- 6" cardboard cake circles (one for each candlestick)
- Aluminum foil
- Small straight pins
- 1 package silver sequin star shapes

Haunted Hint

For pumpkins that get a mask, first place mask on pumpkin and mark where the eyes will be. Cut holes out that are larger than mask eyeholes.

Goblin Court Jester

The Jester Collar

instructions

materials

· Hubbard squash
· 1 stone-colored felt square
· 1 black felt square
· 3 frosty green felt squares
· 1/2 yard of 36" wide black felt
· 7 small silver bells
· White glue
· Silver candlestick
· 4" cardboard cake circle

1 Cut a diamond shape out of three different-colored felt squares from edge to edge (see Diagram 1, page 106).

2 Lay out in a star shape on top of the 1/2 yard of black felt and pin. Top stitch outer edges of star with black thread. Trim around star-shaped collar edges. Cut an "X" into center through all layers of felt.

3 Stitch 6 of the tiny silver bells onto points.

4 Dip the back of the iridescent sequins into white glue and dot around the top of collar.

The Jester Hat

instructions

1 Cut 12" x 12" x 8" triangle from two green felt squares. Cut a 2-1/2" strip from a black felt square lengthways and pin to the center front of one green triangle. From the back, trim away the black felt to match the point of the triangle. Top stitch black strip on.

2 Stitch the two green triangles together, right sides facing. Clip point and turn right side out.

3 From the remaining black felt yardage, cut two triangles measuring 6" x 11" x 18". Stitch right sides together, clip and turn.

4 Start in front and pin black triangle to cone, wrong sides facing. (This will put the black triangle on the inside of cone.) Stitch. Pull the black felt out

of cone and turn up to form a pointed brim.

5 Add the last silver bell to top of hat and, using white glue, dot hat with iridescent sequins.

6 Cut an "X" in center of cake circle as before and put candle stub in silver candlestick. Slip cake circle and jester collar over it. Place Hubbard squash on top, and add the hat.

Baby Gremlins

You'll find these festive little critters so cute and easy to make that they'll run amok at your Goblin King party!

instructions

1 It's the bottom end of this small, flat, pear shaped squash found in grocery stores that gives our Baby Gremlins such character. Their hats are simply two matching free-hand cut triangles, one from each color of felt. Place right sides together and stitch. On one side, make a second line of stitching 1/4" from the first line. Turn right sides out and insert a piece of florist's wire into the tiny casing formed by the two lines of stitching. Crinkle into a hat shape.

2 Dot with sequins dipped in white glue and let dry. Pin the hat in place on the squash. For the eyes, hot glue in place 2 black-eyed peas.

materials

· Chayote squash (1 per Gremlin Baby)

· Stone-colored and green felt scraps

· Florist's wire

· 1 package iridescent sequins

· White glue

· Dried black-eyed peas

· Straight pins

Banquet of the Goblin King

Banquet of the Goblin King Centerpiece

materials

- Skull Orchard Statue (Page 10)
- Plastic green grapes
- Spanish moss
- White berries on wires
- 1 grape leaf vine

instructions

1 Set statue in place on buffet or table. Line the rim of the statue's bowl with wispy clumps of Spanish moss. Hot glue in place if needed.

2 Lay an Elizabethan ruff on top of the bowl and set a large carved Hubbard squash into it. Pull ruff even.

3 Pin grape leaf vine around back of Hubbard and twine about statue. Wire on a few white berries here and there. Wire green grapes to dangle from statue's bowl.

4 Set up two more Hubbard squash and one white pumpkin just to the right of the statue base. Fill in with leaves, berries, gourds, grapes and moss.

Goblin King Invites

The perfect finishing touch for any party is taking the time to create matching invitations. (Okay, I heard that groan!)

instructions

1 Using the clip art provided, why not make these handsome invitations for party guests? Remember, copy stores are our friends; next time you're there, hug a Kinko's!

2 Have them printed on a nice matching card stock. Fold them. Write time, place and directions inside, seal in an envelope and send 'em!

materials

· Choice of Clip art, pages 114, 115.

Banquet of the Goblin King

Banshee Banners

materials

- 2-1/4 yards 72" wide black felt
- 1-1/4 yards 72" wide frosty green felt
- 3 frosty green felt squares
- 8 stone-colored felt squares
- 20 yards black woven gimp
- 1 package black iridescent sequins
- 4 wood dowels, 1/2" x 36"
- 7 Styrofoam balls, 2"
- 3 spools thin black ribbon, 10 yards each
- White felt scrap at least 18" long
- Sewing machine
- Black thread
- Hot glue gun
- Black spray paint
- Roll of florist's wire

Trumpets aren't needed (even if they are a nice touch!) to announce your next Hallowe'en party. Just use the Pointed Pennant and The Forked Tongue to signal the upcoming festivities.

The Pointed Pennants

instructions

1 Use the Dover Art clip art designs provided (see pages 114, 115) or find your own wonderful designs and have them photocopied onto heat transfer paper at your local copy store. (This is the same paper that transfers designs onto T-shirts; it works beautifully on felt too.)

2 For the larger black and green Pointed Pennant, you will need two stone-colored felt squares, one for each character holding the signs. For the two smaller black pennants you will need two each of the letters (see pages 116, 117) "G" ("**G**oblin")

and "K" ("**K**ing") transferred onto the stone-colored felt.

3 To form the points; fold another stone-colored felt square from the top corner to the straight edge (see Diagram 2-2, page 106). Cut the excess from bottom and along fold line. This will give you two points. Repeat for the third one needed. Do this with a green felt square as well.

4 Fold black felt into five equal layers. On top of felt, lay out a design of two green squares in diagonal corners and the two

printed character squares in opposite diagonal corners leaving approximately 1-1/2" of black felt showing around sides and top of square edges. Add the appropriate felt points at bottom (see Diagram 2-3, page 107).

5 Pin felt edges through all layers.

6 Leaving the same 1-1/2" border, cut around design and through all layers of black felt. Remove pins and four of the black backgrounds and set aside. Return pins to hold felt squares in place.

Hallowe'en Crafts: Eerily Elegant Decor

The Larger Pennant

1 Lay the piece with the designs on top, on the green felt yardage. Pin in place and cut around edge leaving a 3" border. Use a zigzag stitch to sew around all felt edges. Remove pins. Turn the 3" green edge in 1-1/2" to meet the black edge, mitering the corners as you go. Pin and zigzag stitch. With a warm iron, press the green edge flat.

2 Hot glue the black gimp on pennant to hide all stitching, including the straight line where the bottom felt points abut the felt squares.

The Smaller Pennant

1 Lay out the "G" and "K" squares in opposite corners of two black felt backgrounds. Add the bottom point to the "K" and pin all in place. Zigzag stitch around the squares and around the outside edge leaving the top open.

2 Cut six 5" x 3" strips of black felt, three for each pennant. Loop them over and pin to top of pennant: one at each end and one in the center. Zigzag stitch across the top to close and secure loops in place.

3 Again, cover all stitched edges with the black gimp.

The Forked Tongue

instructions

1 The lion motif is from a Dover Art clip art book (see page 118) and was enlarged to an 11" x 17" sheet of transfer paper and ironed onto white felt. Cut it out leaving a thin white border around all edges.

2 Next, cut two 9" x 36" strips of green felt and one 4" x 36" strip of black felt. Also cut one 7" x 20" piece of black felt.

3 Stitch the two green felt strips to either side of the 36" strip of black felt. Press seams open flat and top stitch.

4 Fold in half lengthwise and cut a 17" triangle out of one end.

5 Stitch the other black piece to the straight end, press and top stitch.

6 Fold over all edges to the back, press and top stitch. Twist two strands of the floral wire together and insert in the hem (formed by top stitching) at the top and bottom of the Forked Tongue banner. Hot glue lion in center.

The Poles

instructions

1 Spray paint the wooden dowels and Styrofoam balls black.

2 Insert dowel into one Styrofoam ball and slip other end into top of pennant or loops provided. Add another Styrofoam ball. Cut a 1-1/4 yard piece of thin black ribbon and tie from dowel end to end for hanging. Add other lengths of ribbon to hang down.

3 Insert the last pole into the Forked Tongue and top with the last Styrofoam ball. Add cut lengths of ribbon for decoration. The Forked Tongue banner will need to be wall mounted or thrust into the ground.

Haunted Hints

For all banners, dip iridescent sequins in white glue and sprinkle around the banners so they catch the light.

Whenever you have a design transferred for you at the copy center, ask if they will also iron the design to your project (in this case, the pennant). Their irons get sufficiently hot; our irons at home don't—and it's likely the transfer would be ruined were you to try it at home.

A D' Little Orphant Annie says, when the blaze is blue,
A D' the lamp-wick sputters, an' the wind goes woo-oo!
A D' you hear the crickets quit, an' the moon is gray,
And' the lightnin'-bugs in dew is all squenched away—
You better mind yer parunts, an' yer teachurs fond an' dear,
A D' churish them 'at loves you, an' dry the orphant's tear,
A D' he'p the pore an' needy ones 'at clusters all about,
Er the Gobble-uns'll git you
                Ef you
                    Don't
                        Watch
                          Out!

From "Little Orphant Annie" - James Whitcomb Riley

Banquet of the Goblin King

chapter 3

REVEL OF THE RED IMPS

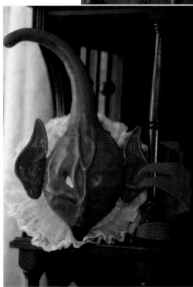

Peering out from all over the room, these deliciously, delightful devils will keep watch over your Hallowe'en party. Make several Imps and tuck them in and about everywhere!

Red Imps

instructions

1 These guys are a blast to make! Use a scouring pad to wash and scrub gourds thoroughly to get off the layer of dirt that clings to them—be sure to get in all the little grooves. Let dry.

2 Decide which side of the gourd would be best for a face; the bumps and ridges will give you a hint. Pencil-in two eerie eyes.

3 Use a 1/8" drill bit to make tiny holes around the pencil line. Also, drill a 1/8" hole in the very tip of the gourd's neck. This will be used later. Carefully "connect" the eye holes together using the X-Acto knife. Carve until smooth.

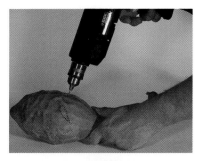

4 Do the same on the backside of the gourd, creating a hole about 1-1/2" across.

5 Clean out the soft, dry pulp from the inside of the gourd using the needle nose pliers. This creates a lot of dust so you may wish to do it outside. If the pulp is in one large piece, carefully break it up until the pieces are small enough to fall out.

6 Now for the ears. Find the perfect location and adhere the ears to your Imp by pushing the pins into the gourd from inside the ear.

7 Close off each ear hole (designed so the human wearer can hear through them) from the inside with a little duct tape.

8 Spray paint the entire gourd red. When dry, over spray with the red glitter paint.

9 Hot glue the pre-gathered lace onto the cardboard cake circle leaving a small area in the center free. Cut a hole in the cardboard center.

10 Align this with the hole in the back of the gourd (as best you can, a perfect match isn't necessary) and hot glue in place. The collar should be slightly higher at the top of the gourd head.

11 Using the pattern (page 111) and instructions (the same for the Goblin King's hands, page 23) create two sets of hands out of the red felt. Spray with red glitter spray.

materials

For each Imp you will need:

· Bumpy "Maranka" gourd (available at craft stores, gourd supply farms or online at Welburn Gourd Farm; see Resources on page 125)

· X-Acto knife

· Needle nose pliers

· Push pins (or map pins)

· Red spray paint

· Red glitter spray

· Black acrylic paint

· 1 yard pre-gathered white lace

· 2 red felt squares

· 1 pair pointed plastic costume ears

· Small Styrofoam heart

· Drill with various bits

· Red thread

· Florist's wire

· Batting

· 7" cardboard cake circle

· Green OmniGlow Lightsticks

· Several small finishing nails

· Duct tape

39

Haunted Hint

Step #3 must be done very carefully or you run the risk of shattering the gourd.

12 Continue by painting the Styrofoam heart black and, when dry, over-spray with red glitter. Stick the head end of a finishing nail into the top dip of the heart. Insert nail into drilled hole in neck of gourd and hot glue in place.

13 Some gourds have a very pointed bottom. Dry brush a little black paint on it for a goatee. Just prior to your party, snap a green Lightstick by OmniGlow and place in the hole in the back of each gourd.

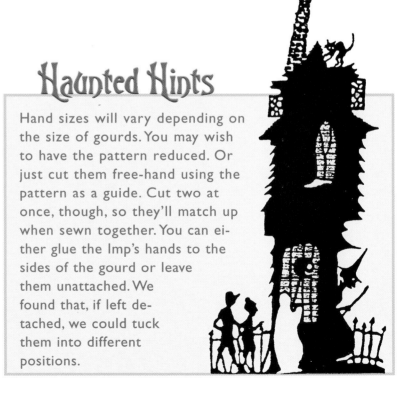

Mark makes a rather dapper devil standing amongst all of his Red Imps.

Haunted Hints

Hand sizes will vary depending on the size of gourds. You may wish to have the pattern reduced. Or just cut them free-hand using the pattern as a guide. Cut two at once, though, so they'll match up when sewn together. You can either glue the Imp's hands to the sides of the gourd or leave them unattached. We found that, if left detached, we could tuck them into different positions.

Brew Some Gruesome Punch Glasses

Napkin/Lid Cover

instructions

1 Create a label by choosing a Hallowe'en sticker or clip art design and adding a slogan made by computer or hand lettering. We used "Demonic Tonic" for ours (see Clip Art 3-1, page 124). Some other ideas we had included "Witches Brew: Good For What Ale's Ye," and "Granny's Ghoul-Aid."

2 Have a local copy store make a color laser transfer of your label and press it onto the center of the 10" x 10" piece of muslin.

3 Lay muslin label over checkered fabric (*wrong* sides together) and top stitch 1" from edges. Use pinking shears to trim 1/2" off of each side.

4 Iron on checkered side to smooth fabric. (Do not touch iron-on label directly with hot iron.) Set aside.

materials

For each jar:

· 1 Mason jar
· 10" x 10" square of muslin
· 10" x 10" square of checked fabric
· 18" twine
· Hallowe'en sticker or clip art
· Waxed paper
· Pinking sheers
· Sewing machine
· Iron

Jars

instructions

1 Fill jars 1/3 full of water and place in freezer until serving time. When ready, fill jar with punch. Cut a small square of waxed paper and place over jar opening. Screw lid onto jar. Cover with fabric napkin, muslin label up. Tie with twine (and a straw) around lid securing napkin.

2 Place in ice-filled chest or very large punch bowl to keep jars frozen.

3 Use the lid cover as a napkin to hold the bottom of the frozen jar and absorb any moisture.

Haunted Hint

For larger jars, label "Brew-4-Two" and add 2 straws.

Red Wax Leaves

materials

· Dried brown leaves (pressed or left to dry naturally)

· Short (or broken bits) solid red candles

· Double boiler

· Aluminum foil

· Waxed paper

instructions

1 Line top of double boiler with aluminum foil for easy cleanup and bring water in bottom part to a boil.

2 Cut candles into small chunks removing the wicks and place in lined top of double boiler. When wax has melted, reduce heat to medium to keep water *gently* boiling.

3 Dip leaves into the melted wax. Be careful not to break them, as leaves are already brittle. Remove and set on waxed paper to cool. Repeat the process 4 or 5 times until desired thickness and color of wax has been reached.

4 Allow unused wax to cool then wrap in the foil and throw out.

Demonic Tonic

Demonic Tonics

The bewitching Bernard Fox, perhaps better known as "Dr. Bombay" in the TV series Bewitched contributed two wonderful recipes with which to fill the Gruesome Punch Glasses.

Punch with a Punch

ingredients

4 quarts dry apple cider (must be dry, not sweet, or else substitute dry champagne)
1 Fifth Orange Curacao
1 Fifth Cognac
1 lemon

directions

1 Mix dry apple cider (or champagne), Orange Curacao and Cognac. Cut lemon in half and add a squirt.

2 Fill Gruesome Punch Glasses and sip slowly—very slowly—or the goblins'll gitcha!

Serves 40

Punch for the Littlest Imps

ingredients

1 quart apple cider
1 quart orange juice
3/4 cup lemonade
1 pint cranberry juice
3 cinnamon sticks
3/4 cup sugar
Slices of orange and lemon

directions

1 Add all juices to a large (30 cup) coffee percolator. In the coffee basket, place the spices and sugar. Perk gently until the flavors meld.

2 Pour into punchbowl and float the orange and lemon slices.

Up to 20 cups

Haunted Hint

For adults, 1 quart rum may be added.

Revel of the Red Imps

chapter 4

THE GRAVEYARD TEA

44

Want to really impress your ghoul-friends this season? Throw a Hallowe'en tea, resplendent with butler.

Tea Table

Burlap Tablecloth

instructions

1 Cut burlap in half and then split one of the halves down the middle lengthwise. Sew the split halves to either side of the remaining half.

2 Measure your table from the center to the floor. Add 4". Fold the burlap into fourths and, using the measurement, cut out a quarter circle. (You may wish to use a piece of chalk attached to string to first draw your line.) Hemming isn't really necessary. Fray the edges or tuck them under the table.

3 Place burlap on table and add the Battenberg topper. Next, put Graveyard Art statue toward the back of table. Edge statue's bowl with mosses and set a plastic Gargoyle on the top.

materials

- Skull Orchard statue (page 10)
- 30" outdoor bistro set
- 5 yards natural burlap
- Round white Battenberg table topper
- Several plastic gargoyles
- Spanish moss
- Reindeer moss
- Sewing machine

Haunted Hints

There are numerous plastic gargoyles on the market today. Some with flashing eyes, others that emit eerie sounds. Carefully spray these with the FleckStone to give them a more uniform look. Before you start spraying them, cover the flashing eyes or tiny speakers hidden in them with masking tape.

Why not make some Graveyard Place Cards by choosing an appropriate bit of clip art and having it photocopied onto card stock? Cut out just the top part and fold over. Write the names of your guests in the space provided.

(See page 113 for art.)

Kasey

Mark

The Graveyard Tea

Pumpkins You Can Take for "Granite!"

46

materials

· 1 FleckStone Spray in Gotham Gray by PlastiKote

· 1 ceramic candlestick

· 1 tudor ruff (page 26)

· One 6" cardboard cake circle

· Candle stub

· Real pumpkin

instructions

1 Hollow out pumpkin from the bottom and carve. Put the candle stub in candleholder. Cut an "X" in the center of the cardboard cake circle and slip down over candle. Place linen ruff on top and put carved pumpkin on top of that.

2 Spray entire piece with FleckStone.

"Ben Bones" the Butler

materials

· Lumber in amounts and measurements given, page 48

· Hammer

· Nails

· Two 2" metal flat brackets

· Screws

· Styrofoam wig head

· Old man mask

· 1 pair pantyhose

· Newspaper (for stuffing)

· Old suit (preferably formal)

· Formal shirt

· Ascot tie

· Suspenders

· 2 wire coat hangers

· 1 pair white gloves

· 1 pair dark shoes

· Plastic tray that looks silver

· Small plastic grocery bag with handles

· Duct tape

· Baby powder

· Drill

· Staple gun

Looking every inch like his favorite dish, "Death Warmed Over," our handy butler is the perfect partner to host your afternoon Graveyard Tea. After all, he's been "residing" there for more than a century!

The Armature

Have your local lumberyard cut, from *two* 2" x 8" x 8' boards, the following amounts and measurements:

One 2" x 3" x 60" length = body
One 2" x 3" x 15" length = shoulders
Two 2" x 3" x 12" length = right arm
Four 2" x 3" x 18" lengths = bottom supports

instructions

1 Nail the support boards (the four 18" pieces) to bottom of body board at right angles so it will stand. Use more than one nail for each board.

2 Place one leg of suit trousers on body piece before proceeding. Nail the two right arm pieces (the two 12" lengths) together at right angles and, using the flat metal brackets, screw to right side of the "shoulder," forming arm.

3 The right hand needs to be able to support a little weight; accomplish this by clipping the hooks off two coat hangers and bending the long, straight edge down, forming a letter "W." Duct tape the cut ends of each hanger together.

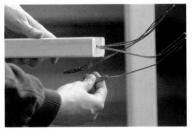

4 Drill two 3" holes in the wooden "wrist" of the Butler. Insert the taped ends of hangers into each hole leaving the "V" part underneath the wrist.

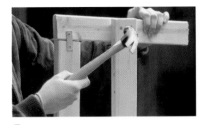

5 Nail the shoulder piece (15" length) to back of body piece in shape of a "T."

6 Stuff the pantyhose with newspaper and duct tape top to the armature. Slip one leg of pantyhose into each trouser leg. Clip suspenders on the trousers to support them from the shoulder bar.

7 Stuff plastic bag with newspaper and place bag handles over both shoulders to form back "hump." Tape in place.

8 Duct tape the Styrofoam wig head to the *front* of the "T" shaped shoulders. This will give the old guy that stooped over, head-jutting-out look!

9 Finish dressing the wooden armature with the shirt, suit and tie, stuffing with newspaper as needed. Do not over stuff, as our Butler hasn't been eating much over the past few decades!

10 Make sure the suspenders are on the outside of the shirt. Duct tape the back of the shirt to armature to hold in place.

11 Place mask over Styrofoam wig head and tuck in around shirt collar. Pin mask to Styrofoam head if needed.

12 Stuff the thumb of one glove (be sure to use the cor-

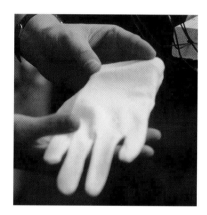

rect hand) and slip it on the wire framework.

13 Tape glove to wrist and pull shirt cuff and coat over it. (The left hand is simply stuffed and pinned inside cuff.)

14 Staple the tray to the wrist to hold lightweight goodies. Add a paper doily to hide the staples.

15 Stand butler in place and cover up wooden supports with leaves and twigs. Place shoes where feet would be and bring trouser legs over their tops. (We added bright orange socks to ours.)

16 Dust with baby powder for a nice, grave-rotted look.

The Graveyard Tea

Hallowe'en Crafts: Eerily Elegant Decor

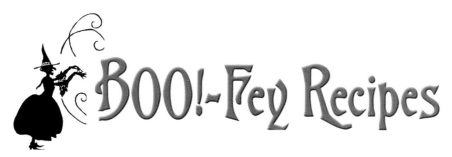

The Graveyard Tea

Spider

ingredients

1 gallon apple cider
1 liter Sprite (or other white soda or pop)

directions

1 **SP**rite + c**IDER** = **SPIDER!** Mix both juice and soda in punch bowl. Add artificial webs and plastic spiders around bowl for effect.

2 Freeze more plastic spiders in ice and float in bowl.

Gargoyle Cookies

ingredients

1 package sugar cookie mix (in pouch)
1 stick of butter (1/2 cup)
1 egg
Two 3 ounce packages chocolate sprinkles
Powdered sugar
Gargoyle cookie cutter (Williams Sonoma; see Resources, page 125)
Flour sifter

directions

1 Prepare cookie dough following directions on package. Cut out cookies but add sprinkles while cookie cutter is still in place; lightly press sprinkles into dough before lifting cutter and going on to next cookie. Place on cookie sheet and bake as directed.

2 For a sharper, more defined cookie shape, here's a little tip: After cookies have baked and have been removed from the oven (but are still hot), reposition cutter over them and press down. Use a small paring knife to help trim away excess dough. Be careful: the cookie cutter will heat up!

3 When cookies have cooled for 2 minutes, remove from cookie sheet and set on flat plate. Sift a very light coating of powdered sugar over the chocolate sprinkles.

Makes 1 dozen.

Stone Cake

ingredients

Pre-made Angel Food cake (or one from mix)
1 pint heavy whipping cream
Powdered sugar
1 package grape, blackberry or orange flavored Kool-Aid
Flour sifter

directions

1 Whip cream until it begins to thicken. Add the package of flavored Kool-Aid and a little powdered sugar. Whip until color is even. Add more powdered sugar to taste. Whip until cream forms peaks.

2 Spread evenly over cake and dust with powdered sugar for a mottled look. Top with gargoyle cookie.

Serves 10-12.

Haunted Hint

Use only powdered sugar when making whipped cream; granulated sugar will quickly turn it to liquid.

Hoot Owl Sand-Witches

Light Owls

ingredients

1 loaf of cracked wheat bread
1 package sliced white cheddar
  cheese
1 package sliced ham
1 package sliced turkey
Honey mustard
Small owl cookie cutter

directions

1 Cut out individual shapes
from bread, cheese, turkey and
ham, using the owl cookie
cutter; a small paring knife
will help if bread doesn't cut
easily. Spread bread lightly
with mustard, and layer cheese
and meats. Top with a final
slice of shaped bread.

Haunted Hint

You can make bow ties
for each sandwich from
red bell peppers.

Dark Owls

ingredients

1 loaf pumpernickel bread
6 fresh basil leaves
8 ounces whipped cream cheese
3 teaspoons sun-dried tomato/pesto
  sauce
Small owl cookie cutter

directions

1 Mix 3 teaspoons of tomato/
pesto sauce into cream cheese.
Finely chop 6 basil leaves and
add to cream cheese mixture.
Spread evenly on bread slice.
Top with additional slice.

2 When cutting out owl shape,
press cookie cutter firmly into
sandwich and trim away edges
with small paring knife.

The Graveyard Tea

chapter 5

THE MANY FACES OF JACK

Upon arrival in this country, early Irish immigrants found that carving the native American pumpkin into wicked, glowing faces was much easier than their European turnips and beets.

The Legend of Jack O'Lantern

Long ago in Ireland there was a man named Jack. A meaner, more conniving, more spiteful man never lived. When he died, those in Heaven had no use for him and those in Hell were afraid he'd take over, so Jack was doomed to molder away on Earth forever.

Before he left Hell, however, the Devil, having been impressed by Jack's less than civil life, gave him a hot coal from the Official Furnaces to light his way.

But the coal was too hot to handle, even for one with a heart as cold as Jack's. So he pulled up a turnip, hollowed it out and placed the coal inside!

Thereafter, every time a strange glow was seen over the marshes, people would know that it was the ghost of mean old Jack. And they began calling him "Jack-of-the-Lantern."

During their harvest cele-brations, the ancient Druids would build great bonfires in celebration and extinguish the fires in their homes. Then they would carry a hot coal in a turnip back to their house to rekindle it. They also carved faces in their turnips to allow more light to shine out and scare away evil spirits.

In many countries, Jack O' Lantern is also known as Will o' the Wisp.

The Hallowe'en Tree

materials

- 8' dead tree (or large limb)
- One 2" x 6" x 6' board
- Saw
- Hammer
- Nails (both small and large)
- Several carved, pie-size pumpkins (we used the customary 13 in ours!)

instructions

1 First off, choose a tree with as many intricate, yet strong branches as you can find.

2 Secondly, if you want to bring your tree inside, make sure this treasured specimen of dead shrubbery that you've found will fit through your door and into your living room—you'll note from the picture, ours did not! (Remember last Christmas when you had to remove four feet from the bottom of your tree AND cut the spire off the top?) Cut tree base level.

3 Now that that's out of the way, saw two 2-1/2' lengths from the 2" x 6" piece of lumber. Then saw the remaining piece in half. Nail the 2-1/2' pieces into an X shape and nail one of the 6" pieces onto each end so it sits flush to the ground. Get the longer nails

Conjured up from the Ray Bradbury story of the same name, comes this glowing, leering Hallowe'en Tree. After all, why should Christmas be reserved for all the fun?

started into the center of the X and nail it to the base of the tree. Stand the tree up.

4 Drive small nails into the tree branches near a "fork." Nestle a small, carved pumpkin into the fork and secure by puncturing it onto the nail. Be sure the pumpkin sits firmly on the branch. Repeat with as many pumpkins as you think your tree will hold.

5 Place larger pumpkins around the tree base in a pile to hide the stand. Secure with nails if needed.

6 We lit our pumpkins with candles, but a string of electric lights would work as well.

Notice the pumpkinseed used as tear drop.

Tom Foolery and His Country Cousin, Buster Britches

materials

· Various hats
· Old white dress shirts
· Bow ties
· Pumpkins
· Large, flat cans (such as tuna comes in)

directions

1 This year, why don't you dress up your Hallowe'en pumpkins in *your* very best finery? We used an old straw boater and an old pop-up top hat from a torn down theatre in New Orleans.

2 Cut collars from old dress shirts and button around the tuna can. A snappy bow tie finishes off this custom look.

Haunted Hint

The monocle on Tom Foolery is a chipped camera lens we secured with straight pins and a decorative chain.

Two Clever Cousins to help you say "BOO!" These guys will rattle both brains and bones!

Rusty Stix and Black Masque Jacks

materials

- Small pie pumpkins 6" to 8" in diameter
- Black glitter
- Straight pins
- White glue
- Black polyester lace 5" to 6" wide (1 yard per pumpkin)
- Black thread
- Needle
- 6" cardboard cake circles (1 for each candlestick or lamp base)
- Thin black ribbon (two 18" lengths for each pumpkins)
- Apple corer
- Plastic ice cream scoop
- Instant Iron by Modern Options
- Instant Rust by Modern Options
- Various candle sticks
- Pumpkin Preserver

Glowing yellow eyes peer out dramatically from behind glittering black masks.

The Many Faces of Jack

The "Rusty Stix" Bases

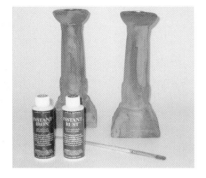

Follow the instructions on the Instant Iron and Instant Rust to coat the candlesticks; let dry.

Haunted Hint

Lamp bases that take small night-light size bulbs also make good bases. Remove the shade and bulb. Put bulb through an "X" cut in the center of a cardboard cake circle and replace bulb. *Do not cover this cake circle with foil!*

The Ruffs

instructions

1 Measure 1 yard of lace per pumpkin. (Larger lamps may need up to 1-1/4 yards.)

2 Using the white glue, trace a simple pattern in the lace. Dust with glitter and set aside to dry.

3 Once dry, use needle and thread to hand gather along one edge of lace. Pull together, leaving a center opening of about 3" in diameter. Stitch ends together.

The Pumpkins

instructions

1 Hollow out the pumpkins from a 3" (no larger) hole in the bottom. Now, use the ice cream scoop to clean out his guts so that he's but a shell of his former self.

2 Even though there are so many books, kits and patterns out today on pumpkin carving techniques, I prefer to carve these jack o' lanterns in a much more simple way, allowing their individuality to shine through in the way they are decorated. Cut out eyes with the apple corer. (Since these pumpkins are rather small, eyes are about all they need.)

3 Add a small hole at the top back of the pumpkin for excess heat to escape.

Kasey found the perfect pumpkin!

The Masks

instructions

1 Using the white glue, draw a mask shape around the eyes of the jack o' lantern. Fill in with more glue, spreading it with a small paintbrush so it doesn't get too thick. Dust the glue with a healthy layer of black glitter. (Do this over newspaper and recycle your left over glitter!) Set aside to dry.

2 Cut two pieces of black ribbon about 18" long. Pin each piece to the pumpkin at the sides of the mask. Pull the two ribbons to the back of the pumpkin head and tie in a bow. Your black glitter mask is now "tied on" securely.

3 Make beauty marks on your pumpkins with a dot of glue and black glitter.

4 To assemble the Black Masque Jacks, place a candle in holder, followed by the foil-covered cake circle, the black lace ruff and finally, a pumpkin.

Haunted Hint

Instead of lace, place paper French leaves (real leaf shapes that are photocopied onto paper found at many cooking stores) on top of the cardboard circle and around the base of the pumpkin. Or make your own by photo-copying leaves out of your back yard.

The Many Faces of Jack

Pumpkin Finials

materials

· Assorted natural wood finials with round bases and pointed tops

· Acrylic paint in orange, green, yellow and black

· Clear acrylic sealant

· Small paint brushes

· Paper cups with handles

instructions

1 Poke the screw end of the finial into the bottom of a paper cup with a handle. This allows for easy handling and for it to sit upright while being painted.

2 Paint finials to look like small jack o' lanterns wearing witches hats. When dry, spray with clear sealant.

3 Replace the actual stems on pumpkins with the finials by breaking off the stem at its base and then screwing the painted finial in its place.

62

Cats 'n Jacks

Yet another heirloom "kreep-sake" for you to make!

materials

- Plastic jack o' lanterns or cat head treat buckets
- Absorbent brown paper towels
- Flour
- Water
- White glue
- Harvest Orange spray paint
- Black spray paint
- Green acrylic paint
- Orange acrylic paint
- Craft paintbrush
- 1 package emery boards
- Orange Lightsticks by OmniGlow
- Thin gauge bailing wire
- X-Acto knife
- Matte finish spray varnish

63

Once popular during the early part of this century through the 1940s, paper pulp jack o' lanterns, cat heads, skulls and devils today command a high price in the antique stores. Many didn't survive because people actually put lighted candles in them.

The following project uses plastic trick-or-treat buckets and safe, non-flammable light sticks to achieve the same, haunting look of "long-ago."

The Garland

instructions

1 For the garland, seven jack o' lanterns, one larger than the others, are needed. Using the X-Acto knife, carefully cut out the eyes, noses and mouths of the plastic pumpkins.

2 Mix 1 part flour with 1 part water in a large bowl. The mixture should not be too thick or too runny … just nice and "soupy!" Add several ounces of white glue for durability.

3 Tear the paper towels into thin, uneven strips. Dip the strips in the flour/water mixture and begin applying them to the plastic jack o' lanterns.

4 Try to keep as much of the molded plastic detail showing. The papier-mâché does not need to be more than one or two layers thick. Cover all sides, including the bottom, leaving the top open. Fold thin strips into the cut-out edges. Allow to dry.

5 Spray paint the jack o' lanterns orange. With a dry brush apply the green paint lightly to the base of the jack o' lantern and a little around where its lid would have been. You may wish to add some detailing to the eyebrows. Let dry.

6 Use emery boards to rub away some of the dried paint in areas that would have been heavily handled through the years such as the top, around eyes, etc.

"Pumpkin" is an English word dating from the mid 1600s. It was derived from the Greek word pepon, which means melon. The pumpkin is a fruit that is related to cucumbers and chayote squash as well. For more fun with the chayote squash, see Baby Gremlins under the Banquet of the Goblin King section (page 31).

7 Spray with the matte finish varnish.

8 Make 2 holes on either side of the jack o' lantern with an ice pick. Insert a 12" piece of bailing wire through the holes

of each jack o' lantern and bend up to form a handle.

9 Snap a Lightstick and place inside each one.

10 Leaf garlands, berry vines or bare branches would all form a great garland base for these old fashioned luminaries.

These can also be displayed individually by hanging them from various tree branches or used to hold treats.

Kasey's costume adds style to the papier-mâché jacks on a garland made of cornhusks.

The Many Faces of Jack

Found on the cover of *Comfort Magazine*'s October of 1925 issue is a lady hanging papier-mâché pumpkins over a doorway. Believe it or not, there was a time when people would actually put a lighted candle in these—not a good thing! Did you catch the resemblance this picture bears to the one of Kasey on page 65?

Hallowe'en Crafts: Eerily Elegant Decor

Dead Pumpkin's Society: School Ghouls

materials

· White pumpkins
· White parsnips
· 3 yards cheesecloth for each pumpkin

instructions

1 Hollow out pumpkins and use an apple corer for the eyes and nose openings. Push a parsnip through the nose hole. Light with Lightsticks or candles.

2 Propped up with a collection of antique books, these guys look very smart indeed!

3 Give your school ghouls floating, diaphanous bodies by swathing them in white cheesecloth for an even eerier effect.

These School Ghouls will make a great project for any teacher. "Freckles the Cat," our feline mascot with the unearthly glowing eyes, appears in the background.

Of ghosties and ghoulies
And long legged beasties
And things that go bump in the
    night!

Haunted Hint

Parsley makes great "hair" and a nail or ice pick used on a pumpkin's surface makes great "freckles."

Potted Pumpkins

68

materials

· Clay pots
· Clay saucers
· Assorted glass and silver compote dishes
· Assorted vines and berries
· Votive candles
· Aluminum foil
· Small to medium size pumpkins

directions

1 Open pumpkins from bottom and scoop out "innards" with an ice cream scoop. Carve face.

2 Pull off a small piece of foil, roughly 6" wide. Fold in half forming a square. Set a votive candle in middle and wrap foil up sides. Flair foil out at top. Set the votive in clay pot and light. Set pumpkin on top and work in your trailing vines and berries.

3 Place other carved pumpkins in silver or glass compotes and candy dishes.

4 Be sure to store the tops of the candy dishes until after the holiday; they *do not* make clever hats for a lighted pumpkin!

Clay pots make great pumpkin bases. Nestle a pumpkin in a clay pot with some trailing vines and leaves as if Mr. Jack just grew there!

Pumpkin Preserver

Here is a new product to keep our favorite masterpieces from sprouting gray hairs and rotting too soon. Once you've carved, just spray all exposed cut edges with Pumpkin Preserver. Then spray the inside thoroughly and turn over to drain and dry. It's that easy (see Resources, page 125).

The Many Faces of Jack

chapter 6

WICKED WREATHS

This lively fellow has his roots in tradition and history. In years past, when a down-on-his-luck traveling man would come across a better dressed scarecrow in a field, or one whose clothes had been washed clean in the rain, he would exchange his own ragged clothing for the scarecrow's better garments. That is why so many scarecrows always wore such tattered attire (not that they started out in Sunday's best by any means).

Scarecrow Wreath

instructions

1 First things first: tightly wrap duct tape around a small area on the wreath and saw clean through it, duct tape and all.

2 On the sewing machine, sew the 1/3 yard of fabric into a tube lengthwise, leaving the ends ragged. Turn rights sides out and feed onto the wreath like a sleeve.

3 Using a little of the polyester fiberfill, stuff the fingers of the yard gloves loosely (so they remain somewhat limp) and slip them onto the taped ends of the wreath. If needed, add a little more fiberfill into the gloves but the wreath alone should fill up the "palms."

4 Hot glue the wrists of the gloves to the straw wreath and pin them in three or four spots to keep them in place. You will never retrieve these pins so make sure the points are well-seated in the straw!

5 Bring the sleeves down over the yard gloves. Remember, your scarecrow can look a little ragtag. If you need to split your seam to get it back over the glove, do so.

6 Shove a bunch of the excelsior mixed with a little Spanish moss up the sleeve. Secure with hot glue if needed, and tie the end off with a piece of roping. Fray the rope ends. Do this for the other glove as well.

7 Interlace the fingers of the gloves together so the scarecrow can hold things in his hands. Add a little hot glue to keep the fingers together.

8 Now for the head: cut two circles from the muslin about 10" across. This will act as the "bag" that the head is made from. Stitch the two pieces together, leaving a small opening to turn it inside out for stuffing. (If you want a more ragtag look leave it wrong side out and fray.)

9 Add a little hot glue around the head's opening and set it on the wreath at the top and just a little forward. Add quilting pins around it to hold it in place. Quilting pins work well in the back to keep the head from falling forward.

10 Next, cut a strip of the muslin about 18" long and 6" wide. Fray one of the long sides and gather the other on a needle and thread. Put it around the base of the head to act as the collar of the "bag." Secure with the thread and some hot glue. Add a piece of the roping and some excelsior around the knot.

materials

- One 14" straw wreath
- 1/3 yard checked fabric (old quilt pieces work great)
- 1 pair off-white cotton yard gloves
- 1/2 yard sturdy, off-white muslin (for head)
- 2 yards small roping
- 2 squares mottled brownish/green felt
- Fabric paints
- 1 skein of black DMC floss
- Natural excelsior and Spanish moss
- Quilting pins
- Duct tape
- A little polyester fiberfill
- Straw basket jack o' lantern or other holiday decor
- Various and sundry autumn bits and leaves
- Sewing machine
- Thread
- Hand saw
- Hot glue gun
- Pair of needle nose pliers

11 For the face, take a needle and thread and go in where one eye would be, pulling it out where the other eye will be. Go back through and pull the thread. This will form a nose and indentations for the eyes. Go back in with the needle and come out where the mouth would be. Push the needle back through the mouth (about 1/2" away) and out the *top* of the *back* of the head. Pull a little until you are happy with the depth of the mouth. Tie off.

12 Use the fabric paints (or buttons) to create the eyes. Use the DMC floss to sew a few big X's for the mouth. These same X's can be used around the side of the head as if that's all that's holding him together. A little blush on the cheeks is a nice touch.

Note: no matter how many times you make this face, it will always come out looking different.

13 Now, he needs a hat. Take the two felt squares and cut out two triangles using as much of the felt as possible. Sew the two triangles together around the two longest sides. Cut a few notches out of the bottom brim and start to stretch the bottom out of shape. The brim will curl slightly and ripple. Cut a few more notches out of the middle of the hat, turn up the front brim and put the hat on the scarecrow's head. Add some excelsior into the notches and secure all with hot glue.

14 At this point, the Scarecrow becomes more of a floral arrangement. Put the wicker basket jack o' lantern in the Scarecrow's hands. Add autumn leaves, berries and a few well-placed bugs (I used small spiders and a couple of lightening bugs).

15 Fill in any bare-looking areas with more excelsior.

16 Other things like Indian corn, acorns, small Hallowe'en decorations and vegetables are great Scarecrow selections.

Note: never use a lighted candle in your Scarecrow's hands!

Haunted Hints

Try using old brown corduroy and purchased leather elbow patches as an alternative to patchwork fabric sleeves.

You may wish to hang three scarecrows on the dining room wall near the table. These could hold silverware or condiments or candies or … ?

Here is a friend who has been sitting out rotting in a field all season. What makes him absolutely adorable is his ever-resilient smile and happy face.

Glass Goblin Wreath

materials

- 1 oval shaped grapevine wreath
- Box of 6 medium sized orange glass Christmas ornaments
- 4 sprays of 1" black glass balls on wire stems
- 4 sprays of 1-1/2" black glass balls on wire stems
- 2 sprays of 1-1/4" olive green glass balls on wire stems
- 3 sets brass comedy and tragedy charms
- 1 package florist's wire sticks
- Green velvet leaves
- Green floral tape
- Black paint pen

instructions

1 Separate all the 1" and 1-1/2" black glass balls, and then wire both sizes together into 4 separate "grape" clusters.

2 Remove hangers from orange balls and hot glue all the balls to the wreath as seen in the photo. Make sure the openings on the orange balls do not show. Tuck the black "grape" clusters about and secure with hot glue.

3 Remove green balls from their wires and sprinkle about the wreath. Glue in place.

4 Separate green velvet leaves and hot glue in and around to conceal any bare spots and wires.

5 Use the paint pen to draw jack-o-lantern faces on the orange balls.

6 Next, cut 3 floral wire sticks in half and bend one end into a small loop. Wrap tightly with green florist's tape. Now,

bend loop to a right angle and wind the rest of the wire tightly around the handle of a thin paintbrush or pencil creating a "vine." Hot glue the looped end onto the top of each glass jack-o-lantern for his stem. Create additional wire tendrils by following the procedure above.

7 Hot glue masks so they peek out from behind leaves and glass balls.

Haunted Hint

Paint the jack-o-lantern faces after balls are in place to ensure they look outward.

Quick-Fix Berry Vine Wreath

Here's a quick and lovely autumn decoration that can be left out until it's time to put up Santa and his elves.

Wicked Wreaths

materials

· 14" grapevine wreath
· Several sprays of autumn berries
· Several strands of raffia tie (about a yard long)
· Hot glue gun

75

instructions

1 If the berry stems have leaves, first remove them and set aside.

2 Wire berries to the bottom of the grapevine wreath. Bring them farther up one side than the other.

3 Tuck the leaves in and around the berries and secure with hot glue. Save a small cluster with a leaf or two for the top.

4 Tie the raffia into a bow and hot glue underneath the wreath.

Haunted Hint

For a frosty autumn look, we applied a very light spritz of bottled snow most often used only at Christmas.

SUNDRY "WITCH CRAFTS"

76

A bewitching assortment of frighteningly festive
things to make.

Hallowe'en Crafts: Eerily Elegant Decor

Instant Ancestors

Hallowe'en is the perfect time to dig up a few friends and old family members to aid in the celebration. These New England-style headstones are just the things to transform your front yard into a perfect Gothic "garden."

materials

- 1 Styrofoam sheet, 18" x 36"x 12" per stone
- Two 1/2" wooden dowels
- One 2" x 4" x 72" board
- One 16" Styrofoam ring
- 1 package small "L" brackets
- Flour
- Water
- Large mixing bowl
- Newspaper
- Serrated knife
- Saw
- Non-stick skull shaped cake pan
- Small screws
- Reindeer moss
- Black acrylic paint
- Olive green acrylic paint
- Sponge
- Fleckstone Spray by Plasti-Kote in Gotham Gray (1 kit will do approximately 1-1/2 headstones)

instructions

1 For the tombstones above, use the serrated knife to round the tops of two of the Styrofoam sheets. This will give you the typical tombstone shape. For the tombstone with the skull face, we based the shape of the stone on an actual one from the 1600s (check old books and websites for more ideas).

2 Use a permanent marker to draw in your inscription and design. If your word runs off the line, don't panic, even stone cutters back then used to continue the word on the next line. Next, press the butt end of the permanent marker into the Styrofoam to "engrave" your design. Go over the groove several times to deepen it.

3 Keep in mind that too many words make the following papier-mâché part more difficult.

4 In a large bowl, mix two cups flour with one-cup water. Work out the lumps until the paste is

the consistency of thick soup adding water or flour as needed.

5 Tear newspaper into strips, 2" or 3" wide and about 12" long. Use only sections with lots of black and white—no colored ink (this will save time trying to cover it up later).

6 Dip newspaper strip into paste. Squeeze out excessive paste by sliding between two fingers and apply paper to Styrofoam, carefully working into grooves. Always overlap your strips. A second layer may be applied for added strength, but too many layers will mask your design.

7 Cover the entire front first and set aside to dry. Afterwards, do the back and sides.

8 If the insides of some of your grooves are too hard to paper, "paint" them with just a thick coat of flour/water paste. If there is a space that is too soggy, place a dry paper strip over area to absorb the paste.

9 To make the skull, layer papier-mâché strips inside the cake pan, smoothing carefully into facial features. When dry, take skull out of pan and place on headstone. Use small papier-mâché` strips to secure. Let dry.

10 Once the "stone" has dried, it will be much sturdier. Now, take it outside and spray it with the Fleckstone. Since the newspaper already makes it shades of gray, good coverage should not be a problem. Set aside to dry.

11 To "age" your headstone, dilute the black paint with water and dip a sponge in it. Squeeze the sponge over the top of the headstone so that the paint rains down on it (a spray bottle works as well). Also sponge some black paint into the grooves of the letters to define them.

12 Sponge on diluted olive green paint for moss. Only do this on one side as moss only grows on the north side of a

stone! When this is dry, hot glue the Reindeer moss over the top, sides and into some of the grooves. Be careful not to obscure the lettering.

13 To stand them up, cut 8" lengths of wooden dowels, two for each headstone, and pound them gently into the ground about 12" apart. Carefully work your headstone onto the dowels. (We found that wooden chopsticks work really well for this, too.)

Haunted Hint

If you place the tombstones on a slight angle and fill in with dirt and debris they will look even more realistic!

Tombstone designs such as winged skulls, cherub faces and hourglass shapes were very popular in centuries past.

78

The Gaelic Cross

instructions

1 Cut two 10" pieces off the 2" x 4". Using the "L" brackets, screw a piece to each side of the main post, 10" from the top.

2 Lay the cross you've made carefully on top of the Styrofoam ring and trace cut lines. Cut out the excess pieces. Use white glue to secure the ring pieces to the cross. When this is dry, papier-mâché as above. Cover all parts of the cross.

We found that wrapping the paper strips from underneath and folding them over the top worked best.

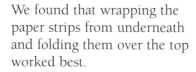

3 Fleckstone, paint and add moss.

4 To stand the Gaelic cross, dig a small hole and bury it at a slight angle, packing the dirt around it.

Haunted Hint

Several ounces of white glue added to the paste will give it extra strength.

Witch Clips

materials

- Six 1-1/2" green glass Christmas balls
- 6 clothespins (the "doll making" kind)
- 1/2 yard black felt
- Batting
- Cream colored acrylic paint
- Black acrylic paint
- Orange acrylic paint (fine nose applicator for writing)
- Green acrylic paint
- Hot glue gun

80

instructions

1 Paint the legs of the clothespins with the cream colored acrylic paint. Allow to dry.

2 Paint the thin lines of the socks with the orange paint and the shoes with the black. Let dry.

3 Hot glue all the glass balls onto the tops of the clothespins with their openings to the top and slightly back. Pull off a small tuft of batting and glue the *part you are holding* to the top of the ball, hiding the opening.

4 Cut the felt into 5" x 5" squares. Fold back one corner and wrap it around the head, overlapping it in the front. Secure with hot glue. Pull up on the pointed corner a little to form her hat.

5 Put two dots of black paint on the ball for eyes (pull up and out slightly at the corners). For the nose, add a small "blob" of green paint—only this time, while squeezing the tube pull up, leaving a point. Let dry. Use to affix your dinner guests' napkins to the sides of their glasses.

Haunted Hint

It helps to have a thin-edged piece of cardboard or plastic box nearby to clip witches to while drying.

Kitchen Witch Night-light

materials

- Plastic Mrs. Butterworth's bottle
- 4 wooden ball doll heads
- 1 yard pre-gathered, 1/2" wide or less off-white lace
- 1 yard thin black flat braid
- 1 square black felt
- Shaped wooden plaque
- Orange acrylic paint
- Black acrylic paint
- Cream acrylic paint
- Small plastic cauldron
- Single bulb electric Christmas candle
- Spider (or other Hallowe'en) confetti
- White glue and hot glue
- Black thread (needle)
- Drill with 1" bit
- Small hand saw

Ever wonder if there was something creative to do with those really great Mrs. Butterworth's bottles? Well, wonder no more! With a wave of your magic hot glue gun you can turn her into a syrupy-sweet old witch to light up your Hallowe'en kitchen.

Sundry "Witch Crafts"

1 From the top of the Mrs. Butterworth's bottle, break off the yellow ring that once held the lid in place. Soak the bottle in warm water to thoroughly clean the inside and peel off the labels. (If the label is being stubborn, a little WD-40 should do the trick!) Wash off any sticky residue that's left. Carefully drill hole in the bottom center of Mrs. B.

2 For the base: Sand all edges of your wooden plaque. Hot glue the four wooden balls to the underside to act as "legs." Paint plaque top and underside (including the four balls, but leaving the edge unpainted for the moment) with the orange acrylic paint. Let dry.

3 Using a ruler, draw diagonal lines across the top of the plaque with a pencil, and then repeat, crossing from the other

Haunted Hints

We found that coloring the pencil lines with a felt tip marker first made the painting a lot easier!

If you have a glasscutter, remove the base of a glass Mrs. Butterworth's bottle for an even warmer glowing light; and use glass paints to decorate.

side to form a diamond pattern. Paint every other diamond black. Paint the plaque edge black.

4 Next, paint her apron, apron ties, and collar with 2 coats of cream acrylic paint. Let dry.

5 Affix the lace to the edge of the apron with hot glue. Then top with the flat braid. Edge her collar with the flat braid.

6 Use the white glue to apply the spider confetti to her apron and add 1 spider to her collar. When dry, paint tiny orange dots on her apron, collar and the 3 buttons down her "blouse."

7 For the hat: Use the bottom of an appropriate sized glass to draw a circle on the felt. Cut out two of these and hot glue together. Whip stitch the edges. Fold this in half and cut a small slit in center. Fold in half in the opposite direction and cut another slit. This will give you an "X" shaped opening. Make this opening large enough to fit over the mouth of the bottle. Cut away the points formed by the slits to make a rounded opening. Set aside.

8 Use the needle and thread to gather the "pre-gathered" lace tight enough to fit around the mouth of the bottle. Glue this around the base of the bottle's mouth so the lace lies on her hair.

9 Glue hat brim on top of the lace.

10 Fold a corner of the black felt over onto itself, forming a triangle approximately 2" long at the base. Cut this triangle from the felt, slightly rounding the bottom. Whipstitch the triangle together to form a cone. Trim the base of the cone to fit snugly over the mouth of bottle.

11 Pull cone right side out and glue in place on brim. Glue a small piece of the flat braid around cone where it meets the brim.

12 Place the bottle and the cauldron on the wooden plaque to get an idea of where to drill the candle hole. Remove bottle and cauldron and drill from the *top down*. Lightly sand edges of hole and touch up paint if needed.

13 Remove bulb from plastic candle before beginning this next part. Break off plastic base from candle and un-knot cord. Insert into bottom of bottle, up to her waist. Add 1/2" and mark. Remove from bottle and carefully saw away what's not needed. Be careful not to cut that cord in there!

14 Insert the candle from bottom of wooden base and hot glue into place. Return the bulb and set your transformed Mrs. B. down over it. Do not glue her down; being able to lift her up is the only way you'll be able to change the bulb! Do, however, glue the cauldron into place.

15 For "steam" in the cauldron, tuck some lamb's wool into the pot.

Corn on the Cub Night-light

materials

· 1 bamboo #5 knitting needle (3.75 mm.)
· 1 large-eyed needle
· 1 skein orange cotton yarn
· 1 skein yellow cotton yarn
· 1 skein white cotton yarn
· 4 wooden ball doll heads
· Oval wood plaque
· Orange acrylic paint
· Drill with 1" bit
· Single bulb electric Christmas candle
· Small bag of candy corn
· White glue
· Small bowl
· 3 small honeybee shaped buttons
· Small wooden bucket
· Hot glue sticks for wood

What bear cub wouldn't give up honey when surrounded by such a Hallowe'en treat? All ready for bed in his nightcap, our Candy Corn Cub will glow all night to keep the goblins at bay.

Candy Corn Cap

instructions

1 Cast on 24 stitches yellow:
Row 1 Knit.
Row 2 Purl.
Repeat through Row 8
*Row 9: Decrease 1 stitch.
Knit row.
Row 10 Decrease 1 stitch. Purl row.
Row 11 Knit.
Row 12 Decrease 1 stitch. Purl row.
Row 13 Decrease 1 stitch. Knit row.

Row 14 Purl.
*Row 15: Switch to orange yarn. Continue pattern from * (Row 9) through * (Row 15) until there are 10 stitches left.

2 Switch to white yarn. Continue above pattern until 1 stitch remains on needle. Cut yarn about 6 inches long and pull through remaining stitch.

3 Fold cap, right sides together, and whipstitch together with yellow yarn first, then orange, and then white following the colors of the cap.

4 About 1/2" before white is completely closed, pull dangling white thread through the cap turning it inside out. From outside continue closing the white tip with needle and yarn.

Pompom

Instructions

1 Cut 1-1/2 yard lengths each of the yellow, orange and white yarn.

2 Hold the ends of all three yarns between thumb and forefinger. Wrap the yarns around first and second finger (releasing thumb) until all yarn is wrapped. Tie one 6" strand of white yarn around

the thread between your fingers. Tighten and knot.

3 Carefully slip your forefinger out of loops and slip scissors in to cut the yarn.

4 Trim all yarns (including 6" piece used to tie) until pompom is a small and smooth ball.

5 Thread needle with white yarn still attached to end of cap. Stitch through center of pompom and secure, leaving a 2" length of yarn between the pompom and the tip of the cap. Trim end of white yarn the same length as pompom yarns.

The Assembly

instructions

1 Empty out honey from honey bear and wash thoroughly. Discard the cap.

2 Drill a 1" hole in the middle of the wooden plaque and in

the bottom of the honey bear. Set bear aside. Hot glue the four wooden ball "feet" on the bottom. Paint entire base orange.

3 Break the plastic base off of the electric candle. Carefully cut the plastic candle (watch that cord!) so that it and the bulb will stick up through the hole in the base about 2", or

until it is even with the honey bear's tummy. Hot glue in place.

4 Set bear down over electric candle and draw a faint line around his base. Again, remove bear. Set the base on wax paper.

5 In a small bowl, combine white glue and candy corn and mix thoroughly. Begin "globbing" the candy corn/glue mixture onto the top of the base, piling it high in some areas and trickling off the edge in others. Be sure not to cover the line where the bear will sit. The glue will dry clear and seal the candy corn at the same time.

6 When dry, remove base from wax paper, add light bulb (we used an orange one), set bear in place and put on his cap.

Here's the Scoop on Candy Corn …

Candy corn is still made the same way today (practically) as it was more than a hundred years ago! Spokespersons for the Goelitz Confectionery Company (the same fun people who bring you all those flavored Jelly Belly brand jelly beans) tell us that a wooden tray is first filled with cornstarch. Then a wedge-shaped metal form gets impressed into the cornstarch. The mold is then filled up, one squirt at a time, with the three different colors. It's left to sit around for a day or two and then the candy is separated from the cornstarch. The misshapen pieces are sorted out and discarded and the rest goes off to be packaged.

The Goelitz candy people have been doing this non-stop since 1898!

Did you know that twenty million pounds of candy corn is sold each Hallowe'en? That works out to be almost nine billion separate kernels!

But we can get candy corn pretty much all year long. It comes in red, white and pink for Valentine's Day, red, white and green for Christmas ("Reindeer Corn") and white with pastels for Easter; yup, it's called "Bunny Corn"—the kids love to put it out to feed the Easter Bunny. And here you thought Santa had all the fun!

Oh, and one more thing, the proper order for the Hallowe'en colors is yellow on the bottom followed by orange in the middle and tipped with a bit of white. (By the way, if you push these onto your teeth they make great fangs … just don't let your mom catch you doing it!)

7 For the honey bucket: write the word "HONEY" on a small wooden bucket. Next, fill it to over flowing with hot glue made for wood (it's yellow) then add a couple of bee shaped buttons to the handle.

Clay Pot Candle Holder

materials

- Small terra cotta saucer
- Small terra cotta pot (size of a votive candle)
- Fimo brand baking clay in Terra Cotta
- Small baking sheet
- Hot glue gun
- Real leaf (with good veins!)
- Moss green acrylic paint
- Sponge
- X-Acto knife
- Pencil
- Cardboard toilet paper tube
- Aluminum foil

86

instructions

1 Hot glue the clay pot to the saucer. Be sure to add a little hot glue inside clay pot as well, letting it ooze through the hole in the bottom. This gives added durability.

2 Pre-heat your oven according to the instructions on the Fimo modeling compound and line a small baking sheet with foil. Cover the cardboard tube with foil as well.

3 Roll out a small portion of Fimo modeling compound, enough to cover your leaf and still be 1/4" thick. Lightly press leaf vein side down into Fimo (we used a rolling pin to be sure we pressed evenly). Trim around the leaf's edges with the knife and discard leftover for another use. Carefully peel the leaf away.

4 Place this leaf over cardboard tube and onto baking sheet. Next, roll a small "snake" of Fimo and twine around a pencil for vine. Bake all (yup, including the cardboard tube and pencil!) as instructed.

5 When cool, hot glue leaf and vine in place (see photo). Lightly sponge the acrylic paint around the edges of the saucer, pot and leaf for added color.

Haunted Hint

Always pick up your candleholder from the bottom; the leaf is for decoration only and not intended to be a handle.

Those Amazing Maize Brothers

Whether prospecting for gold, gambling on a Mississippi River boat, tending the crops or playing baseball in the street, these amazing maize boys always hang together.

Sundry "Witch Crafts"

... except for old Uncle Ned who was hanged for horse rustling!

materials

· Indian corn (with husks)
· Four 1-1/2" Styrofoam Balls
· Small straight pins
· Twigs
· Twine
· Scraps of felt, leather and tiny checked fabric
· Finishing nails
· Hammer
· Felt doll's hat (to fit Styrofoam ball)
· Black acrylic paint in fine tip bottle
· Brown acrylic paint in fine tip bottle

instructions

1 Tear the husks from the ear of corn and soak in warm water. Once pliable (about an hour later) shape husks around the Styrofoam ball and pin to hold. Allow to dry.

2 Lightly tap a finishing nail into the center top of the ear of corn and press the husk covered ball down onto it. Secure with hot glue.

3 The type of doll's hat you choose will indicate what kind of character you'll be making: cowboys, riverboat gamblers, and farmers were some of the best hats we could find.

4 Hot glue the hat to the head. We kept the faces simple. Two dots for eyes, smaller dots for freckles.

5 If necessary, adjust the size of the coat patterns; cut out of appropriate fabric. Machine stitch around the perimeters leaving no more than a 1/4" seam allowance. Make small notches in the armpits up to thread line and turn the coat (or shirt) right side out.

6 Insert a twig into each sleeve and glue "arms" to top of ear of corn *behind* the head. Arrange coat in front and glue down if needed.

7 For the **Riverboat Gambler** (see patterns, page 120) add two paint dot buttons to the back of the black felt tail coat (at the waist) and a black curled mustache. His collar is a 1-1/2" length of corn husk, folded lengthways and wrapped around the nail "neck." Fold the tips down in front.

8 The **Old Prospector** (see patterns, pages 108, 109) has a duster made of leather scraps. Just leave the edges natural. The cape part of the coat is two half circles put together with big "X's" of thread. A leather lash closes his coat around him. The mustache is a piece of yarn tied in the middle and twisted on the ends and hot glued into place. His pipe is a bit of clay added to the end of a toothpick and stuck into the Styrofoam.

9 **Farmer Bob** (see patterns, page 119) only has a small woven check shirt that is hanging in tatters. He's chewing on a tiny piece of wheat inserted into the Styrofoam by first making a pinhole. Roll up his shirtsleeves, as he is hard at work!

10 **The Kid** (see patterns, page 110) has a denim letterman's jacket made from the leg of an old pair of jeans. The waistband is actually the bottom hem, hot glued into place. The letter "C" (for corn) is made with a paint pen. A length of old twine made the perfect rustic scarf.

11 As for **Old Uncle Ned,** well, since he's been gone for some time and hasn't eaten in years we used an old, well dried, eaten ear of corn for him. We draped him in ghostly garments of diaphanous cheesecloth and included the same twine noose from which he was hanged! The skull is a store-bought one.

You may try using old doll clothes (such as those for Ken) for these guys, too.

Hallowe'en Hoop-La

materials

· 10" embroidery hoop
· 1/3 yard black lace fabric
· 1-1/4 yards pre-gathered black lace trim
· 1/8 yard orange felt
· 1-1/4 yards black braid
· 1 small bag potpourri
· 1 pre-made Hallowe'en decoration
· Black fabric paint with pointed tip

instructions

1 Separate the embroidery hoop. Cut two squares of lace fabric and lay one on top of hoop bottom. Spread a thin layer of potpourri inside hoop and on top of lace, removing any large items such as pinecones or other seedpods.

2 Cover all with second lace square and replace embroidery hoop top, securing tightly.

3 Pull lace fabric carefully to make it taut.

4 Trim lace fabric from around hoop edges.

5 Starting on the lower right side (when facing) glue the pre-gathered black lace around the backside of hoop.

6 Trim one long side of felt with pinking sheers. Use the black paint to dot a small pattern near the pinked edge. Cut felt so it is about 2" wider than the black lace trim. Slightly gather with needle and thread and glue on top of black lace in back.

7 Glue the black braid around the front of hoop's perimeter.

8 Next, hot glue your pre-made Hallowe'en decoration in place, covering the lace trim edges.

Haunted Hint

If too much potpourri "sifts" through the lace, "sandwich" in a layer of black tulle on top of the lace.

Spook Nest Inn

materials

- 1 wooden bird house
- 1 package wooden doll house shingles
- 3" x 1/4" x 36" balsa wood
- Wooden doll house window frame with shutters
- Wooden doll house gingerbread trim (for the roofline and eaves)
- Wooden doll house corner molding
- Khaki green acrylic paint
- Cream acrylic paint
- Black acrylic paint
- Small paint brush
- Sponge
- X-Acto knife
- Hot glue gun
- Drill with small drill bit
- Small wood dowel
- Small piece of jewelry chain (the cheap stuff!)
- Small white bird
- Scrap of cheesecloth

90

instructions

1 Okay, gang, this one takes a while (due to preparation), but if you run right out now and get the supplies you need and put the balsa wood pieces outside to weather, it should only take a few weeks!

2 Use the X-Acto knife to cut the weathered piece of Balsa wood into small strips roughly 3/4" wide. Starting at the bottom of the birdhouse, hot glue the wooden strips so they just barely overlap each other like house siding. Get the sides and back done first; on the front you'll want to cut away any slats that cover the opening. Finish off the house edges by gluing a piece of corner molding to all four sides.

3 Next, glue all the shingles on the roof in the same manner (starting at the bottom and overlapping the rows).

4 Glue the window frame onto front center, leaving the shutters for later.

5 Water down the khaki paint and "wash" the roof to give it color. Mix the cream colored paint with a tinge of khaki and dry sponge hints of color on the corners, around the window frame and the shutters and wooden gingerbread fretwork. This gives it that neglected, peeling-paint look.

6 Hot glue all the wooden fretwork in place. Hot glue the shutters to the side of the window opening at angles. We also removed a couple of the slats in the shutters for an even more haunted look.

7 Cut a small rectangle from the balsa wood and paint "Spook Nest Inn" on both sides. Drill a small hole on one side of house, insert the wood dowel piece and hang the sign from it using the scrap jewelry chain.

8 Drape the cheesecloth around the bird and hang or glue to the perch. The wooden mouse on the sign started out as a button.

Haunted Hints

If you want your birdhouse to hang outdoors you're gonna have to spray it with several coats of a matte finish polyurethane.

The bird nest "bedrooms" were created by rolling a little ball of Spanish moss, hollowing out a hole, and making crazy bird tombstones out of leftover scraps of balsa wood. We used names like Jenny Wren, Stool Pigeon, Walter Pigeon and even Here lies Tweety: that's all folks!

Sundry "Witch Crafts"

The Gourd Guys

materials

- Three 6" to 7" diameter gourds (1 with a long curved neck)
- 2 pair children's overalls with snap-crotch opening (6 months to 3T)
- 2 boys' shirts, blue striped and checked (6 months to 3T)
- 1 girl's romper (12 month size) to match boys'
- Six 7/8" wooden buttons
- White thread
- One 14" straw hat
- 1 wheat straw
- 1 old baseball cap
- 3/4 yard red cotton fabric
- 1 bag wooden excelsior
- Two 36" x 5/8" wooden dowels
- 3 small rectangular pieces of wood for bases, roughly 2" x 4"
- Black paint
- 3 wire coat hangers
- 2" wide roll packing tape
- 1 screw driver
- Hot glue gun
- Needle nose pliers
- Saw
- Newspaper (for stuffing)

Sitting in a field of Brown-eyed Susans, these three siblings are enjoying some fine Hallowe'en fun as "little brother" reads from his collection of vintage Hallowe'en books.

instructions

1 Soak and scrub gourds until any dark spots are removed and gourds are left nice and orange. The two boys use the 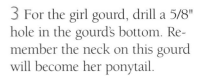 neck of the gourd as their necks and the girl uses it as her ponytail.

2 For the two boys, cut a small square off the bottom half of gourd's neck.

3 For the girl gourd, drill a 5/8" hole in the gourd's bottom. Remember the neck on this gourd will become her ponytail.

4 Empty out loose seeds.

5 For eyes, double a length of white thread and insert into needle making four strands. Stitch an "X" through the buttonholes and tie off. With a drop of hot glue, secure eyes to all three gourds.

6 Add freckles to cheeks by dotting with black paint. Set gourds aside to dry.

For the armatures

7 Measure the overalls and romper from the seat to where the neck would be, add 5" and cut measured lengths from wooden dowels.

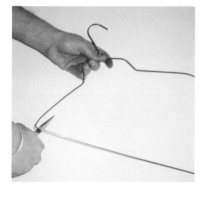

8 Screw or nail flat wooden base to end of dowel. Base will sit front to back for balance. Secure with added hot glue.

9 Shoulders are created by cutting bottom of hanger off on each end as shown. Turn ends down. Straighten hook on top of wire hanger and tape to top 5" of wooden dowel.

10 To dress our Gourd Guys, roll up cuffs of sleeves, if necessary, and stuff with wadded paper. Put shirt on armature and button neck. Unsnap overalls and work base of armature into the open legs.

11 Continue stuffing and buttoning shirt. Bring overall straps up and over and hook. Add more paper stuffing to shirt as necessary.

12 Continue stuffing from the opened pant legs, snapping them closed as you go and leaving the rectangle of wood on the *outside*.

13 For the romper, a small opening will need to be made in the seam where her little "straw" bottom goes. Put the romper on the dowel *before* adding the coat hanger.

14 **Big Brother:** Make a very small hole where the corner of his mouth would be. Insert wheat straw.

15 Clip 1/2" slits around brim of straw hat. Pull and tear brim into a ragged edge. Cut a small hole in the top of hat. Push crown of hat in to form a "valley." Glue to head at a jaunty angle.

16 Insert head onto proper armature (and into shirt collar) using the hole cut earlier.

17 Fray edges of a 16" x 16" square of red fabric. Fold into a triangle and tie around neck for a neckerchief.

18 Stuff wads of excelsior into the arm and leg openings for straw.

19 **Little Brother:** The old red baseball cap is just that. We found this one at a thrift

store and "beat it up" a little more by washing it in a mild Clorox solution then, while still wet, beating it on concrete with a metal meat tenderizer mallet. (If that doesn't take out buried aggressions I don't know what will!)

20 Secure hat to gourd head with a couple of hot glue drops. The bill of cap may be set at any angle.

21 Add a small red handkerchief made from the red striped fabric to his shirt pocket and excelsior as above.

22 **Baby Sister:** For arms, take a wad of excelsior about 6" long. Then, tightly wrap the excelsior with a 1 yard length of white thread about 2" from one end. Secure with a drop of hot glue. Slide the unbound end onto the wire frame and into sleeve of dress.

23 For the bow, cut a 6" x 30" strip of red striped fabric. Fray the edges about 1/4". Fold into a "Z" shape: one end on top, one end on bottom.

24 Cut a 3" x 6" piece of fabric. Slightly gather with fingers lengthwise and wrap around the middle of larger folded piece to form bow. Stitch together in back. Hot glue the back of the bow to the base of the curved gourd neck as shown. Fluff out sides of bow.

Haunted Hint

Using old clothes from your closet, why not replicate your entire family as Hallowe'en Gourd Guys? Set a bushel basket next to them to hold treats for passersby.

94

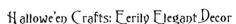

Old-Fashioned Party Fans and Favors

Sundry "Witch Crafts"

Fans

materials

· Vintage cardboard cut-outs or postcards
· Light weight cardboard (like on the backs of legal pads)
· Spray glue
· Wooden paint stirrer (free at Home Depot)
· Orange acrylic paint
· Black acrylic paint
· Masking tape

instructions

1 Take those treasured vintage postcards and cutouts and have them laser copied at your local copy store. Spray mount them onto the cardboard and cut out.

2 Paint the wooden stirrers orange. When dry, "stripe-off" with the masking tape and paint with the black acrylic. Let dry. Remove tape and dot the orange areas with more black.

3 Hot glue sticks to back of decoration and put one at every place setting.

Haunted Hint

If painted lines on the stick aren't sharp, edge with a deeper orange paint from a bottle.

Favors

instructions

1 Use the pinking shears to cut the crepe paper into 10" x 12" rectangles, one for every cardboard tube.

2 Unfold a yellow napkin, gather it from the middle and stuff the point into one end.

3 Fill the tube with candies, trinkets and other small Hallowe'en favors, being careful not to let them fall out the "napkin" end.

4 Stuff another napkin in the other end and roll tube in the black crepe paper rectangle. Secure with a small piece of tape.

5 Cut 2' lengths of orange curling ribbon and tightly tie off each crepe paper/napkin end.

6 Cover tape with Hallowe'en sticker. Or, do what we did and cut out a reduced color copy of a vintage Hallowe'en decoration (or postcard) and tape into place. Our "stickers" match the Party Favor Fans.

materials

- Cardboard toilet paper tubes (1 for each party guest)
- Black crepe paper
- Pinking shears
- Clear tape
- Yellow paper beverage napkins
- Orange curl ribbon
- Old-fashioned Hallowe'en stickers or clip art

Haunted Hint

Not enough toilet paper tubes? Use paper towel tubes cut in half.

Sundry "Witch Crafts"

Canned Hallowe'en

materials

- Unused aluminum paint cans (hardware stores)
- Orange card stock paper
- Halloween designs of your choice (or the ones provided)

98

The can ingredients can be as varied and as clever as you wish. Here is a list of suggestions we found to be just right:

- Candy corn and licorice jelly beans wrapped in netting or cellophane
- A small decoration such as a roll of crepe streamers
- Pumpkin carving kit
- A small pumpkin
- Pumpkin seeds (for next year!)
- A spooky sounds tape or CD
- A copy of a scary poem
- Mask (necessity)
- Vintage noisemakers (find great deals online or at antique stores)
- Disposable camera
- Votive candle (for that pumpkin)
- … the possibilities are endless.

instructions

1 To make the can, use the clip art provided (on pages 122, 123, or some of your own—perhaps a child's drawing) and have it copied onto orange cardstock at your local copy store. It takes two 8-1/2" x 11" sheets of paper to go around each can.

2 Use a quarter as a template to draw a half circle on each piece of paper. Cut out so the bucket's handle will fit easily through.

3 For the lid, we simply printed out the words "Canned Hallowe'en: Everything you need for an instant haunted evening" on the computer and cut it out in a circle shape to fit.

4 Then just fill it up, pound the lid on and deliver to your neighbor; ring their door bell and hide. They'll like this surprise!

Party Hat Lights

materials

- 1 or more package orange children's party hats
- 1 package yellow tissue paper
- String of large bulb outdoor Christmas lights
- X-Acto knife
- Scotch tape
- Scissors
- Stapler

instructions

1 Remove the staples and elastic cord from the party hats. Lay flat face down and, on the backside, draw a pumpkin face. Use the X-Acto knife to cut out the face.

2 Line the openings from the backside with yellow tissue paper and secure with tape.

3 Re-fold the hats and staple back together.

4 Using the scissors, snip the top points off about 3/4" down.

5 Remove a bulb from the string of lights and place party hat shade over it. Replace bulb and repeat.

6 Hang string of lights in the tree branches or over the dining room chandelier.

Haunted Hint

This idea works great for any themed holiday or event, such as birthdays. There's practically a party hat for every cartoon character and TV show out there. Choose your favorite, snip off the end and put the "shades" on the string of lights.

chapter 8

MORE HAUNTED HINTS

HAUNTED HINT #1: Collect things that can be used in your decorating theme throughout the year. Haunt yard sales, antique stores, even the Internet for vintage Hallowe'en goods and decorations. Many may be expensive but there is always a treasure to be found especially in the "off" season (you know, like Easter). We found this old doll dressed in an orange Hallowe'en clown suit.

HAUNTED HINT #2: Tuck old pieces of Hallowe'en themed sheet music or old embossed postcards in your decorations. Big names to look for include Tucks and Brundage for post cards.

HAUNTED HINT #3: Don't spend your entire decorating budget on too many diverse things like a witch here, a black cat there, a skull in the corner. Rather, choose a theme and buy as many items in that scheme as you can, such as pumpkins. Carve them, decorate them, use them for serving bowls, etc. If the budget is very small, spend its entirety on one dramatic arrangement for the buffet or dining table.

HAUNTED HINT #4: Inexpensive sponge rubber bats (3 for $1.00 at Michael's Craft Stores) make great wall decorations. Buy as many bats as you want. Use masking-tape to stick them all over your walls for an instant bat-cave.

More Haunted Hints

HAUNTED HINT #5: Adjust all the pictures on the walls to hang at angles.

HAUNTED HINT #6: Cover furniture with inexpensive white sheets to avoid spills and otherwise messy guests. This will also give your "haunted house" a museum-like, unlived-in look.

HAUNTED HINT #7: Decorating with vintage childhood Hallowe'en books is a wonderful way to add a touch of nostalgia to your Hallowe'en celebration. These are full of harmless spook stories and festive games from yester-year that still hold up well today. Set them on tables or tuck them in displays but most of all read them to your children! What a wonderful way to start new holiday traditions. Old books can be found in antique stores, library sales and, as always, online!

102

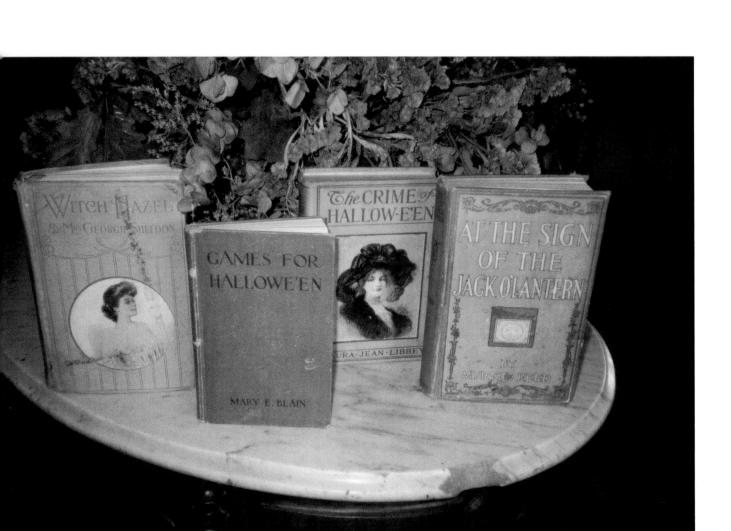

HAUNTED HINT #8: Use grapevine wreaths (alone or decorated with some moss and berries) as plate chargers and trivets under hot dishes. They will spare your tabletop while adding to that Autumn Harvest feeling. Smaller grapevine wreaths can be decorated and used to hold place cards.

HAUNTED HINT #9: Use the decorative lid off one of those large, three-flavored pop-corn tins (with a Hallowe'en design, of course) as a trivet for hot dishes. Adhere four sticky felt circles evenly around the edges of lid. Later use the tin to store breakable decorations or leftover paper plates.

More Haunted Hints

HAUNTED HINT #10:
Vintage photos (your own or others) and magazine covers also make for great holiday decorations. These can be found at many of the same sources as for the postcards and books mentioned above.

Hallowe'en Crafts: Eerily Elegant Decor

HAUNTED HINT #11: Don't forget to look for vintage embossed cardboard decorations from companies such as Beistle (also known as Luhrs). One rule of thumb to remember on some of these cardboard cut outs is that most were only done in three colors: orange, yellow and black. Green was not introduced into many of them until years later.

More Haunted Hints

PATTERNS

DIAGRAM 1
JESTER COLLAR

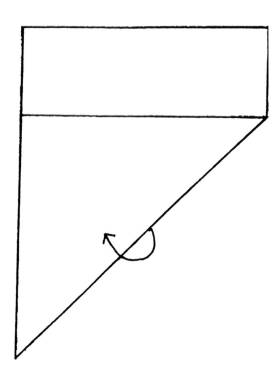

DIAGRAM 2.2
FOLDING THE POINT
BANSHEE BANNERS

Hallowe'en Crafts: Eerily Elegant Decor

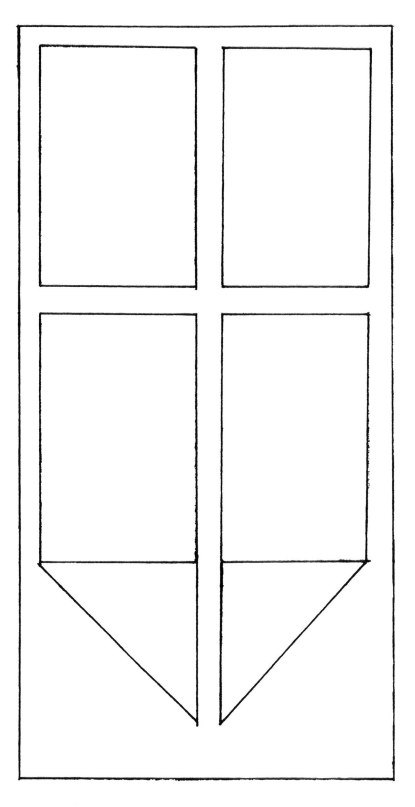

DIAGRAM 2-3
LAYING OUT THE DESIGN
BANSHEE BANNERS

Patterns

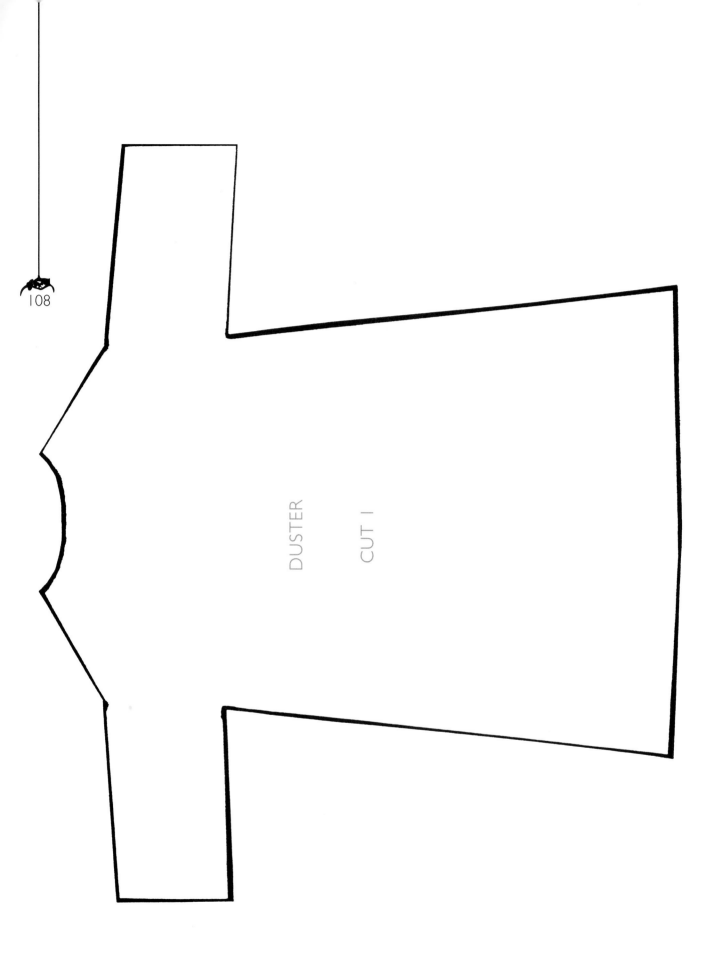

DUSTER

CUT 1

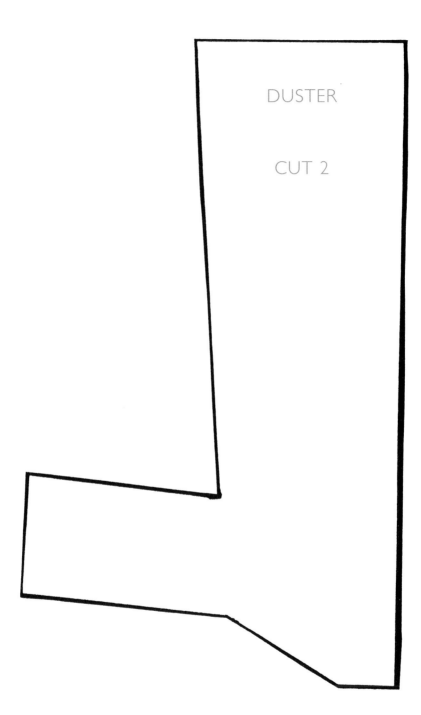

DUSTER

CUT 2

Patterns

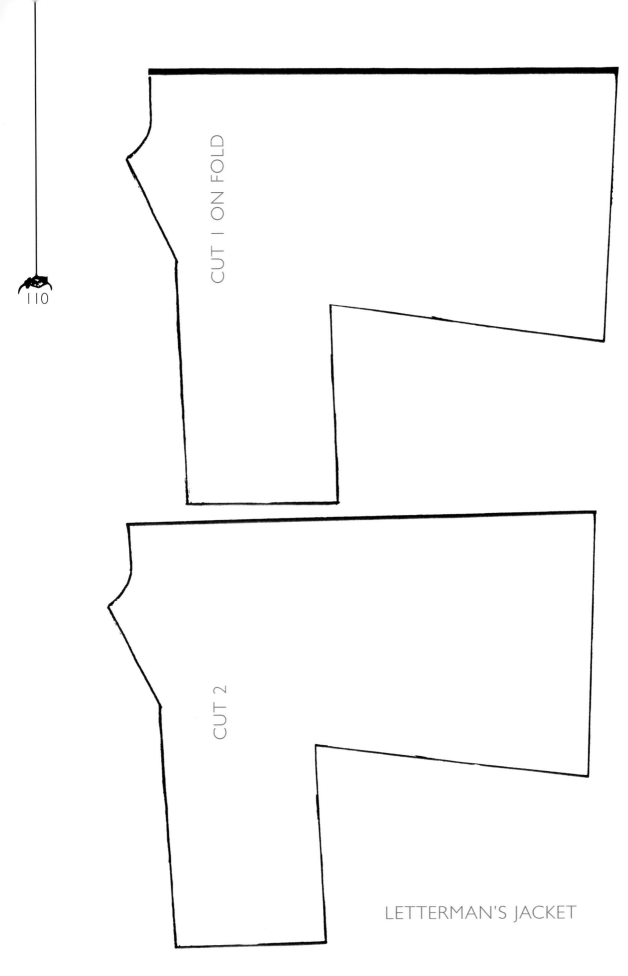

CUT 1 ON FOLD

CUT 2

LETTERMAN'S JACKET

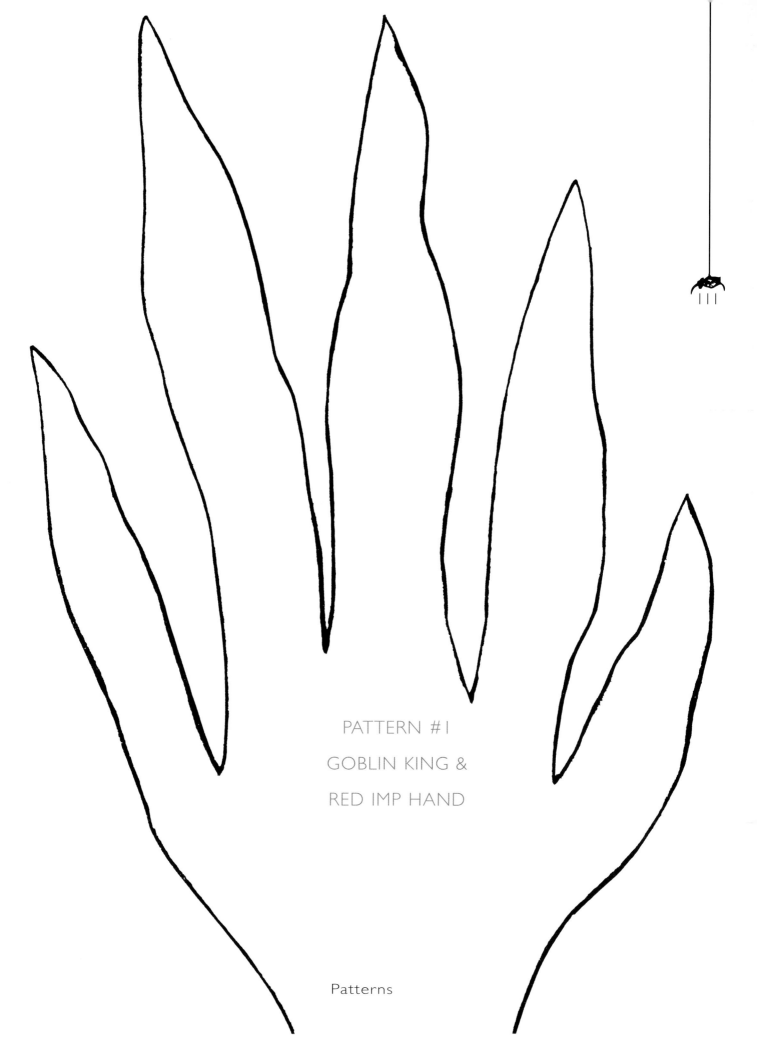

PATTERN #1
GOBLIN KING &
RED IMP HAND

Patterns

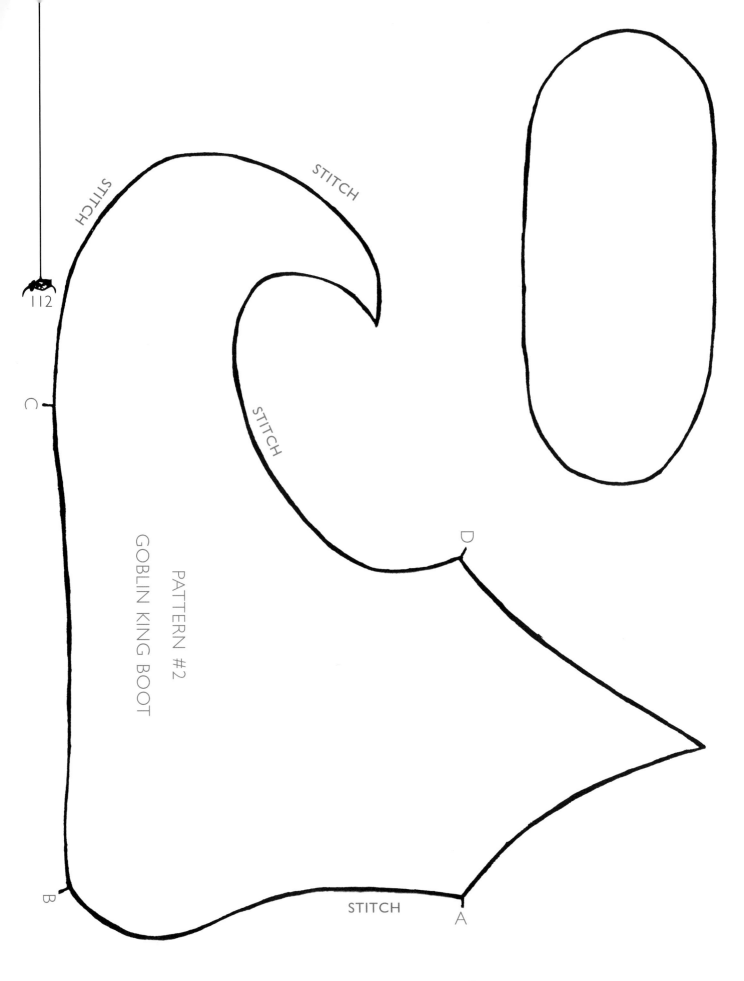

STITCH

STITCH

STITCH

STITCH

C

D

B

A

112

PATTERN #2

GOBLIN KING BOOT

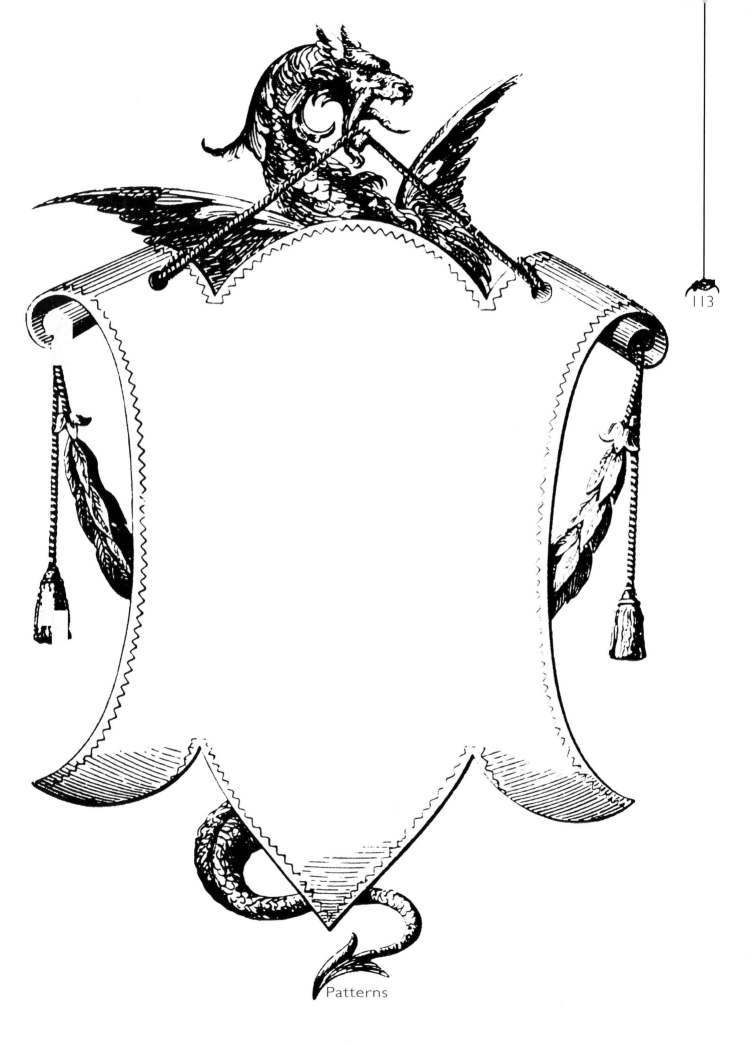

Patterns

Banquet
of the
Goblin
King

Banquet of the Goblin King

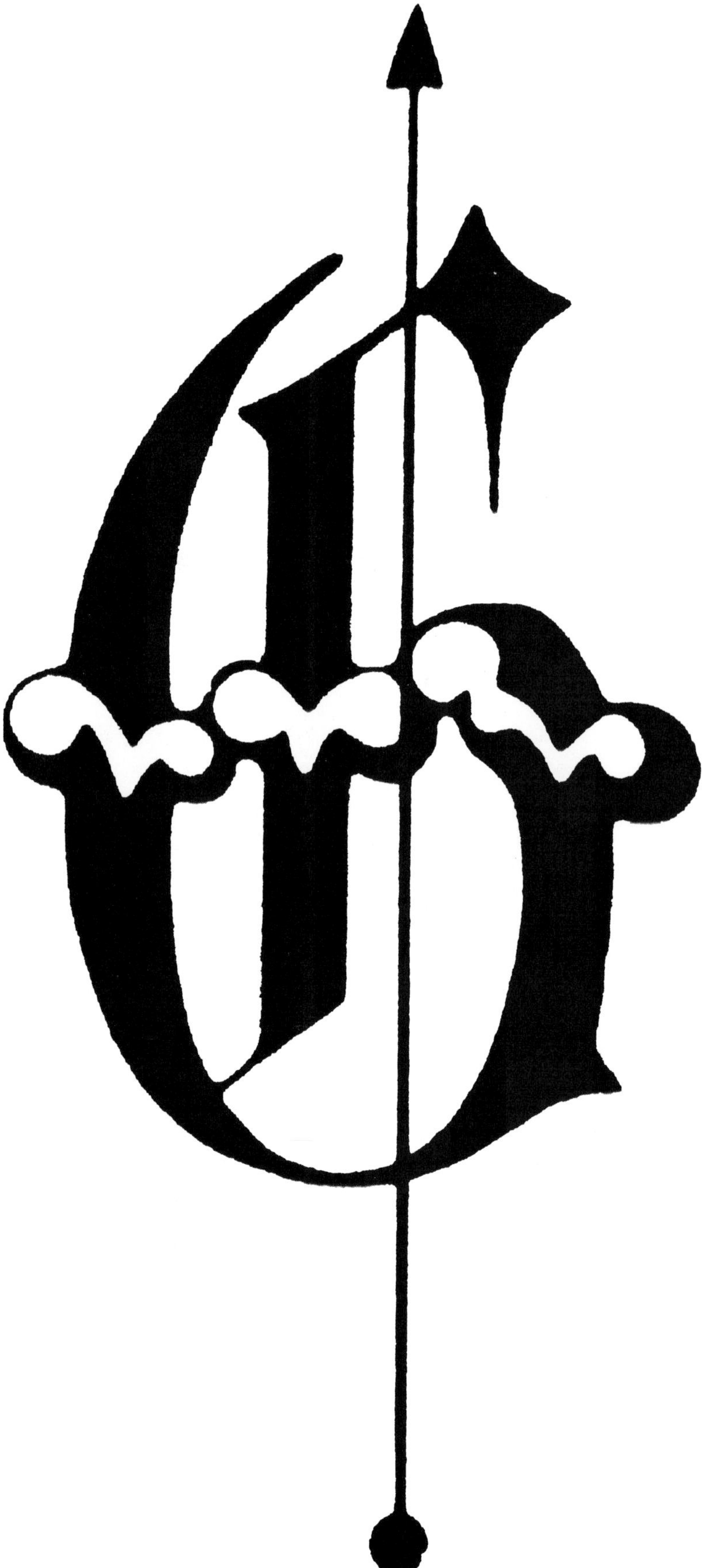

Patterns

Hallowe'en Crafts: Eerily Elegant Decor

SHIRT

CUT 1 ON FOLD

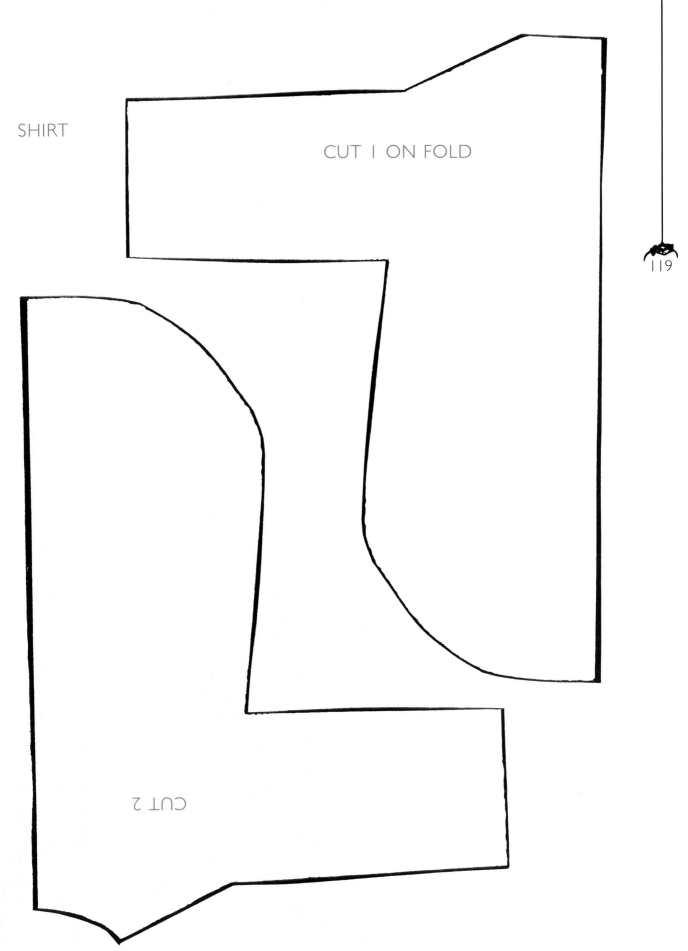

CUT 2

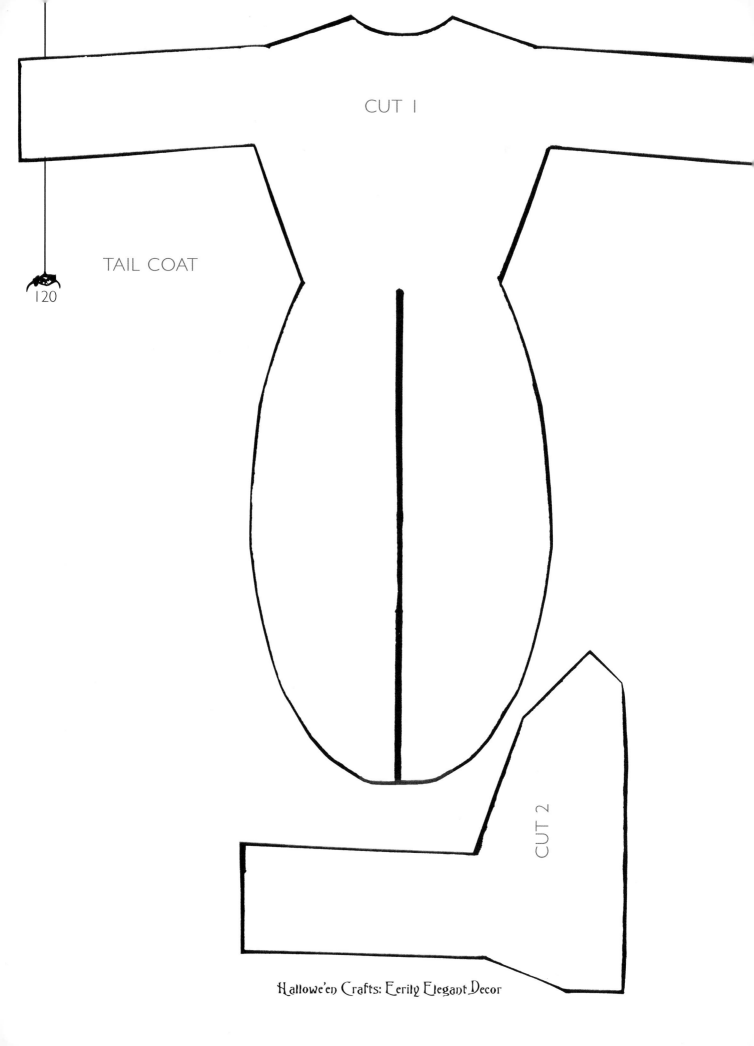

CUT 1

TAIL COAT

120

CUT 2

CANNED HALLOWE'EN

(EVERYTHING YOU NEED FOR AN INSTANT HAUNTED EVENING)

Patterns

CANNED
HALLOWE'EN
(EVERYTHING YOU NEED FOR AN
INSTANT HAUNTED EVENING)

CANNED HALLOWE'EN

(EVERYTHING YOU NEED FOR AN INSTANT HAUNTED EVENING)

CANNED HALLOWE'EN

(EVERYTHING YOU NEED FOR AN INSTANT HAUNTED EVENING)

Demonic Tonic

Locations
The Stagecoach Inn Museum
51 S. Ventu Park Road
Newbury Park, CA 91320
(805) 498-9441

White Meadows Art Gallery
& The Francis Lederer Estate
23130 Sherman Way
West Hills, CA 91307

The Leonis Adobe & Plum-
mer House
23537 Calabasas Rd.
Calabasas, CA 91302

Pointed Ears
Cesar, Inc.
25 E. 21st St. 8th Floor
New York, NY 10010

**Candy Corn and
Jelly Belly® beans**
Herman Goelitz Candy Co.
Solano Business Park
Jelly Belly Lane
Fairfield, CA
Jelly Belly Hot line:
(800) JB BEANS (522-3267)
www.jellybelly.com

Feathers, Feather Boas
Zucker Feather Company
P.O. Box 331
California, MO 65018
(573) 796-2183

Gourds
Welburn Gourd Farm
www.welburngourdfarm.com)
http://www.blessingfarms.com
/catalog.html

Pumpkin Preserver
Jodi Roppoccio
(954) 443-0006

Photocopies
Kinko's Copy Stores
(800) 254-6567

GloLights
Omniglow Corporation
(800) 762-7548
www.glow2000.com

Paints
Plasti-Kote Division (Fleckstone and other finishes)
(800) 328-8044

**DMC Floss, Fimo, Delta Re-
naissance Silver Foil Kit, Instant Iron and Instant Rust:**
Michaels Craft Stores
(800) MICHAELS

Gargoyle Cookie Cutter
Williams-Sonoma
(800) 541-2233 or
(415) 616-7753

Clip Art
Dover Clip Art Books
Dept. 23
Dover Publications, Inc.
31 E. 2nd St.
Mineola, NY 11501

Go Where Your Imagination Takes You

Photo Art & Craft
by Carolyn Vosburg Hall

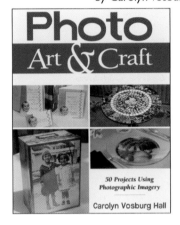

Create, scent, color and embellish professional looking candles at home with this full-color guide. Everyone from the beginner to the intermediate candle-maker will find it easy and rewarding to make their own candles with the step-by-step instructions for pillars, tapers, container candles, mold making and much more. Dr. Robert S. McDaniel is also the author of Essentially Soap, finalist for the 2001 Award of Excellence.

Softcover • 8-1/4 x 10-7/8
128 pages
250 color photos

Item# PHTC • $21.95

The Complete Guide to Glues & Adhesives
by Nancy Ward & Tammy Young

In 1995, Tammy Young's *The Crafter's Guide to Glues* took the crafting world by storm. Now, Tammy has teamed up with Nancy Ward for this full-color follow-up that covers everything you need to know about glues and adhesives currently on the market, including their uses and applications for memory crafting, stamping, embossing, and embellishing any surface. Besides presenting the basics, like safety, there are more than 30 quick and easy step-by-step projects.

Softcover • 8-1/4 x 10-7/8
144 pages
75 color photos

Item# CGTG2 • $19.95

Essentially Candles
The Elegant Art of Candlemaking & Embellishing
by Dr. Robert McDaniel & Katie McDaniel

Create, scent, color and embellish professional looking candles at home with this full-color guide. Everyone from the beginner to the intermediate candle-maker will find it easy and rewarding to make their own candles with the step-by-step instructions for pillars, tapers, container candles, mold making and much more. Dr. Robert S. McDaniel is also the author of Essentially Soap, finalist for the 2001 Award of Excellence.

Softcover • 8-1/4 x 10-7/8
128 pages
250+ color photos

Item# ESCA • $19.95

The Complete Guide to Vintage Textiles
by Elizabeth Kurella

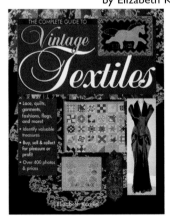

This is the most comprehensive book on identifying, pricing and collecting antique textiles ever. Nearly 500 photos show intricate detail, making identification easy. Also includes more than 400 accurate prices plus convenient lists of dealers, collectors, auction houses and more.

Softcover • 8-1/2 x 11
256 pages
475 b&w photos
16-page color section

Item# ANTX • $19.95

To place a credit card order or for a **FREE** all-product catalog call 800-258-0929 Offer CRB**1**

M-F 7am - 8pm • Sat 8am - 2pm, CST

Shipping & Handling: $4.00 first book, $2.00 each additional. Non-US addresses $20.95 first book, $5.95 each additional.
Sales Tax: CA, IA, IL, PA, TN, VA, WI residents please add appropriate sales tax.

Krause Publications
Offer CRB1
P.O. Box 5009,
Iola WI 54945-5009
www.krausebooks.com

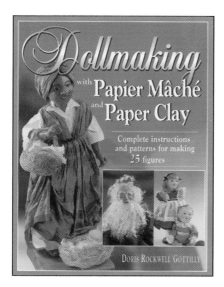

Dollmaking with Papier Mache and Paper Clay
by Doris Rockwell Gottilly

The author shares techniques and knowledge gleaned from 25 years of sculpting experience to help dollmakers fashion unique creations. With clear instructions and step-by-step photos you can create a wide variety of characters. You'll learn to make hair, bodies, armatures, costumes, and how to sculpt heads and faces, arms and hands, and legs and feet.
Softcover • 8-1/4 x 10-7/8 • 160 pages
50 b&w diagrams • 100 color photos
Item# PMD • $22.95

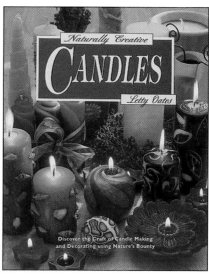

Naturally Creative Candles
by Letty Oates

This unique art form is brought to vivid life as author Letty Oates demonstrates the immense potential of numerous natural materials in making and decorating different candles. More than 250 sharp photos reveal the results of creative candlemaking.
Softcover • 8-1/2 x 11 • 128 pages
250 color photos
Item# NACC • $19.95

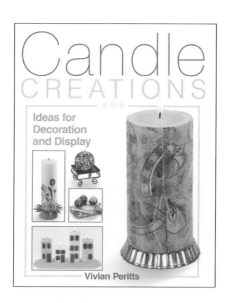

Candle Creations
Ideas for Decoration and Display
by Vivian Peritts

Learn how to quickly and inexpensively change store-bought candles into treasures for your home by using techniques such as adding color, painting, gradation, whipping, softening and twisting. With step-by-step instructions and more than 200 illustrative photographs, you'll be able to recreate the more than 100 beautiful projects with ease.
Softcover • 8-1/4 x 10-7/8 • 128 pages
200+ color photos
Item# CCIE • $21.95

The Good Earth Bath, Beauty & Health Book
by Casey Kellar

In this practical guide to beauty and well-being, you will learn how to make Mother Nature your Fairy Godmother! With remedies and toiletries made with natural, simple formulas and ingredients found in health food, drug, and grocery stores, you can learn how to pamper yourself. The more than 75 formulas-including those for lotions, toothpaste, cough syrup, lip balm, and hair care-will enhance your health and produce spa-quality beauty results.
Softcover • 8-1/4 x 10-7/8 • 112 pages
75 color photos
Item# GEBBH • $19.95

The End